THE ELEMENTS OF
THE I CHING

Stephen Karcher PhD is a writer and lecturer on myth, divination and archetypal psychology, and a personal consultant. He has been working with the *I Ching* for over 30 years. He currently leads Wayfinders, an international association for the divinatory arts, and created the Eranos Foundation's *I Ching Project* (1988–94).

The *Elements Of* is a series designed to present high quality introductions to a broad range of essential subjects.

The books are commissioned specifically from experts in their fields. They provide readable and often unique views of the various topics covered, and are therefore of interest both to those who have some knowledge of the subject, as well as those who are approaching it for the first time.

Many of these concise yet comprehensive books have practical suggestions and exercises which allow personal experience as well as theoretical understanding, and offer a valuable source of information on many important themes.

In the same series

> **the elements of**

the i ching
stephen karcher

ELEMENT

Shaftesbury, Dorset • Rockport, Massachusetts • Brisbane, Queensland

First published in Great Britain in 1995 by
Element Books Limited

This edition published in 1996 by
Element Books Limited
Shaftesbury, Dorset SP7 8BP

Published in the USA in 1995 by
Element Books, Inc.
PO Box 830, Rockport, MA 01966

Published in Australia in 1995 by
Element Books Limited
for Jacaranda Wiley Limited
33 Park Road, Milton, Brisbane 4064

Reprinted 1997

Cover design by Max Fairbrother
Typeset by Phil Payter Graphics
Printed and bound in Great Britain by
Biddles Limited, Guildford and King's Lynn

British Library Cataloguing in Publication
data available

Library of Congress Cataloging in Publication
data available

ISBN 1–86204–035–4

CONTENTS

Acknowledgements

The author would like to thank the Eranos Foundation, Ascona, Switzerland for its support of the *I Ching Project* (1988–94), Rudolf Ritsema for collaboration and preliminary research, Luise Scharnick, Jay Livernois, Brigitte Heusinger von Waldegge, and Ian Fenton of Element Books, my intelligent and long-suffering editor.

FOREWORD

Thirty years ago I was walking down a cold, rainy street, not knowing where I would go next. I was alone, emotionally and spiritually in exile. I turned into a strange little bookshop to get out of the rain. There I saw a grey book with Chinese writing on the cover, and an irresistible voice spoke to me. That was the spirit of the *I Ching*. Later, when I used it, I experienced what it was to ask a book a question and get the kind of answer that said: 'I see you. I am concerned with your welfare. I care how you live and how you die.'

This book, which we could call 'The Little Book of Knowing What to Do', offers you quite a bit more than the version I found. It is based on the practical experience of thousands of people who use the oracle as an imaginative tool, and it draws on decades of new research into sinology, archaeology, depth psychology and the history of religions. It is a new way of looking at a very old book.

Today, more and more people are turning to 'other' ways of interpreting themselves and their problems. We are using tarot cards and runes, chanting mantras, consulting fortune-tellers and becoming witches. Everything that used to be viewed as superstition and the work of the devil is returning to haunt us. Or, perhaps, to save us. The *I Ching* is a part of this. Consulting an oracle and taking its answers seriously puts you into contact with what has been repressed in the creation of our mechanized and de-personalized world. It puts you back into what the ancients called 'the sea of soul' by giving you advice on what sort of actions and thoughts lead to the experience of imaginative meaning. This is the heart of magic. Our interest in old ways and other cultures is a reflection of how much we need to recover this kind of meaning. The *I Ching* can speak to you on many levels and you can think about it in many ways. The magic occurs when, at a particular moment in your life, you ask the spirit for an image to guide you.

STEPHEN KARCHER

INTRODUCTION

What is the *I Ching*?

The *I* (pronounced 'ee') *Ching* is an oracle. It is a 3,000-year-old book that was originally invented in order to talk with gods and spirits. In contemporary language, it offers a way to deal with the problems you confront by keeping in touch with the *tao* or 'way', the creative basis of life we now call the unconscious. It lets you see into difficult situations and connect with the hidden energies that are creating them. It can give you advice on how to live connected to both inner and outer worlds. It can help you find your 'way' in life.

How it works

The *I Ching* is a set of 64 divinatory figures. Each one is made up of a name, a six-line graph or hexagram, and a group of short oracular phrases. These divinatory figures are a dictionary of the hidden forces that move and change things. They act like mirrors for the unconscious forces shaping any problem or situation. In traditional language, the *I Ching* 'provides symbols' which 'comprehend the light of the gods and spirits'. When you ask it a question, it produces an answer that can 'reach the depths, grasp the seeds and penetrate the wills of all beings under heaven'. Listening to this voice enables you to work in harmony with the *tao* or way and the hidden spirit of the time.

The spirit of the time

We don't just live in a world regulated by mechanical time. We don't live in that world in our dreams, or in the kind of knots and difficulties that we encounter during our individual lives. These reflect another kind of time. This 'other time', like our dreams and the world they come from, is full of spirits.

Whether you are aware of it or not, these spirits can and do influence you. They belong with you, and they continually create situations that force you to become aware of them. This reflects a fundamental principle of the creative imagination. In each knot or difficulty that entangles us there is a spirit trying to communicate, the 'spirit of the time'. The oracle is there to give you specific, practical advice on how to connect with it. The idea is that you will be happier, and things will go better for all concerned, when you act in accord with this spirit rather than working against it. When you do so, time becomes special, meaningful, filled with life.

'Special' time

The dictionary defines time as 'a non-spatial continuum in which events occur, an interval on that continuum, and a system by which intervals are measured or reckoned'. This is 'clock time' or 'scientific time'. All the units are interchangeable. That's the point: one minute is no different from any other minute, one date is no different from any other date. But there is another kind of time. We can see it in the way we talk: troubled times, good times; in your own time, the right time, in the nick of time; the time of your life, the moment of truth; make time, do time, before its time, behind the times, time out! This kind of time has a very different quality, one that depends on the individual person involved.

This is how time works for the oracle. It always has a special quality dependent on who is involved, on who asks the question. The oracle doesn't tell time like a clock. It leads you into a story of the time that puts what is going on 'inside' together with what is going on 'outside' in a meaningful way. This is 'living time', and it reflects the way things happen in the soul.

The working of the oracle

You don't just read the *I Ching*; you ask it a question and you get an answer. The answer comes through what your conscious mind sees as 'chance'. You pick six coloured marbles out of a basket, throw three coins six times, or divide and count out 50 yarrow-stalks. This 'chance' event lets something else do the choosing. It lets the spirit of the time get around your conscious control and pick out one of the oracle's symbols to give you an answer. This is what C G Jung called 'synchronicity'; a kind of time and meaning that are not just cause and effect. You, your situation, the 'chance occurrence' and the answer chosen are all part of a special quality of time. The *I Ching* uses this special time to give you a mirror of what is going on 'behind the scenes' in your life. What you normally think of as a chance event opens up the dialogue.

The meaning of *I Ching*

I Ching means 'Classic of *I*'. The word *ching* or 'classic' comes from about 200BCE when five 'classic books' were established in China. The book was known by a different name, *Chou I*, before that time; *Chou* is the name of the kings who were said to have first used the *I*, about 1100BCE. It also means 'to include everything, to go in a circle', so *Chou I* means 'Encompassing *I*'. The important word is '*I*'. Usually the book is simply called *The I*.

You have probably seen *I* translated as 'change' or 'changes'. It really means a particular kind of change, when something strange or out of the ordinary is occurring. It tells you what you can do about this kind of change: be fluid, dissolve your fixed ideas, don't get stuck, let yourself be moved and changed by the hidden spirits. In one version, the Chinese word has the picture of a lizard or chameleon in it. In another, it has the picture of the sun and a negative sign that also means 'moon'. The word *I* was also used to mean 'give a gift to someone'. We can put all these elements together to produce something like this: *I* makes you aware of how things are moving in the moonlit world of the soul. It is a gift to humans. Through it you can change colour and move like a chameleon. You don't have to get stuck in your problems.

What *I* is really about is imagination. The symbols of the *I* describe the way spirits are moving the imagination, spirits that are the 'seeds of events' in the world. The book connects you to these spirits and to your own *I*, your creative imagination, if you choose to use it. Those 'heavy problems' become gifts of the spirits, invitations to a dialogue with *tao*.

The origins of *I*

We don't really know where *I* came from. But we do know that it grew from a desire to talk with the spirits. Many of the words of the book are at least 3,500 years old, and they were part of a special language called *I* used by diviners and developed in the royal houses of ancient China. This language grew from an even older shamanic tradition of songs, stories, chants and spells which were 'accessed' through a system of **whole** and **opened** lines that eventually became the hexagrams.

About 1100BCE, Wu Hsien, the 'Conjoining Shaman', put together the words, the lines and a way to consult them through counting yarrow-stalks. This was called the *Chou I*. Legend says it was used by the kings of the *Chou* Dynasty to overthrow their corrupt predecessors, establish harmony and keep in touch with the *tao*. People outside of the ruling family began to use the *Chou I* or Yarrow-stalk Oracle about 500 years later, during what is called the Warring States Period. This was a time of social breakdown and change that was both very chaotic and very creative. Society was falling apart, much like our own, and individuals needed the oracle's advice. About 200BCE, at the start of the Han Dynasty, a group of scholars made the *Chou I* into a *ching* or classic. They codified the writing and the oldest texts, collected the new material developed during the Warring States Period and put it all together. The *Chou I* became the *I Ching*. The book as we know it is virtually the same as the text they produced over 2,000 years ago. In one way or another it was used by everyone in traditional China, from government officials to street-corner diviners. Images from the *I Ching* were the basis for poetry, philosophy, magic and popular literature. Its roots in ancient shamanism and magic connect it with traditional cultures all over the world. The text is still used today as an oracle throughout the East.

Communicating with the spirits

The *I* grew out of the landscape, history, myths and dreams of northern China. It presents a beautiful, mysterious and complex world full of people, animals and mythic creatures engaged in every kind of activity imaginable. It incorporates a whole series of social and political changes, from prehistoric into historical times. But the language that the old diviners and shamans developed to talk with spirits made it into something unique. It became a world of symbols that describes the way the imagination moves and changes. The tradition says that these symbols were spontaneously produced by magicians and shamans to connect with the 'living world', what we call the creative unconscious. We need information about some of the symbols in order to use them. But using them gives us access to something that is bigger, wider and deeper than any specific culture.

Neo-Confucianism

Neo-Confucianism is an official interpretation of the oracle developed by China's ruling class. It says there is a hierarchical order in the world: heaven above, earth below, men above, women below, rulers above, ordinary people below, and the *tao* or way is to submit to this order. This is a later, political, 'upper class' interpretation. The oracle's symbols are older, more interesting, more popular and more creative than that. We, who can step outside such a hierarchical system, can read them as imagination, not history, and release the oracle's power.

In the same way, we can read all the 'gender' and 'power' words in the *I Ching*, such as wife and husband, king and commoner, as roles that the imagination is continually working through. It is what the figure is doing or how they are acting

5

that counts. You can 'husband' today and 'wife' tomorrow, act like a king in relation to one problem and like a labourer in relation to another. You are, potentially, all these things. They are roles you step in and out of in the course of your imaginative life.

This is the difference between this *I Ching* and most other versions. This version leaves the moral and political system aside. It makes the symbols themselves available to you again, just as if you were consulting a real diviner rather than a government-sponsored interpreter.

Divination

Divination isn't just fortune-telling. It is about finding and contacting what is hidden in yourself and in the world. It was used all over the ancient world to keep in contact with unseen forces. The basic idea is that we ask the gods or spirits – the 'spirits of the time' or *tao* – to tell us what they want and how they are moving. This gives spirit a chance to talk to you now, here, in the events of your daily life. It isn't morality, either. The symbols in a real divinatory system don't have just one meaning. Divination is a creative way of contacting spirit, of perceiving forces in the imagination and inventing ways to deal with them. It opens a space where these spirits can involve themselves in your life.

Talking to spirits

What the old world called spirits are 'inner beings' that modern depth psychology calls 'complexes'. We like to think that we 'have' complexes. But if you look deep enough, you soon see it is really the other way around; complexes really 'have' us. What we call 'complexes' are more than just leftover parts of what we think and feel. They are centres of power in the imagination that create what we experience as 'real'. The Greeks called these complexes *daimon*, a word that means 'provider or nourisher'. They give you what you need to exist. Talking with these 'inner beings' and spirits heals, helps and empowers people. It gives them access to the great ocean of images and stories that the *I Ching* calls the way or *tao*. It is

6

true we can't use symbols, magic ceremonies, sacrifices and myths as if we belonged to a tribal or a traditional culture. What we can do is realize that these things express something real about our psychology and our imagination. They help us in what we can call 'soul-making', acting in accord with soul, spirit and imaginative reality rather than destroying it.

The magic of the *I Ching*

Anything that deals with the 'special kind of time' is magic, because it gives you access to the 'spirit world'. But it is a particular kind of magic. You can't use it to control other people or change the weather. You can use it to become aware of and act in harmony with those 'others' that you meet in your dreams every night. It can make you happier, more effective, more compassionate and more imaginative. You can act with a deeper knowledge of things. In the long run, it can change the way you see the world.

Think about it this way. You want to do something and make plans. Then you feel strange and uneasy; you sense there is something going on. You need to know what the 'other people' in your psychological household think about what you want to do. You want to know whether the time is right to do it, and what sort of attitude or strategy would be most effective. Those 'others', the spirits or complexes, can either help you or seriously interfere with you. They know about things you are not aware of because they are where all your stories, images, motivations and desires come from. They can warn you, redirect you, encourage you, give you instructions on how to go about things, or forecast disaster. The oracle opens the dialogue with these spirits, and the result of that dialogue is what the old shamans called *shen ming*. It means 'bright spirit' or 'intuitive clarity', 'daimonic and clear-seeing' or 'the light of the gods'. It is an awareness of the *tao* or way.

The meaning of *tao*

The word *tao* means 'way' or 'path'. Think of it as a great stream of living energy which permeates everything, and which moves and shapes the world. *Tao* offers a way or path for each individual thing, and is the fundamental idea in Eastern thought. Where Westerners argued about logical definitions of what is real, Chinese argued about what the way is and how to keep in touch with it. It is the difference between saying 'I will find a way to do what I want' and 'There is a way for me and I want to find it'. In terms of *tao*, it is the world that gives you the answer, not the other way around. Those things we tend to think are of primary importance – success, power, money, security – are secondary to finding your 'way'. Some said that *tao* means a particular set of social rules. Some said it is a continual process in the imagination, a kind of shamanic journey. Some said it is 'doing nothing' (*wu wei*), not initiating action but waiting until it is suggested by spirits or circumstances. Everyone agreed that keeping in contact with this 'way' is the most important thing we can do. The oracle was developed to help you do it, by giving the *tao* a voice.

To be 'in' *tao* is to experience meaning. It brings joy, freedom, connection, compassion, creativity, insight, love. Someone who wants to live their life in accord with the way, and uses the oracle to help them, was called a *chün tzu*, literally 'child of the chief', the most important thing. The *chün tzu* doesn't just acquire money, power and fame. She or he acquires *te*, the power to manifest *tao* in action and become who she or he is inherently meant to be. For the *chün tzu*, the oracle is a sacred vessel, what was called a *ting*. It is the symbol for a continual process of transformation.

Like 'spirit', *tao* moves in mysterious ways. It seems to work like psychic energy, accumulating, moving suddenly and unpredictably, undermining things that have become rigid and stiff. It works through imagination, too, and dreaming is a good analogy of a dialogue with the *tao*. Working with the oracle is like an amplified, intensified, focused dreaming, one that can respond directly to your problems and concerns. It helps you practically in the short run, and spiritually in the long run.

Connecting with *tao*

The first thing you need is a question. This question should grow out of a problem that you can't solve in the usual way, one that acts like a hidden centre, drawing energy and attention. This problem shows where the spirits are moving in your soul. Look for the characteristic feelings: anxiety, desire, resistance, the sense of something hidden or confusing, the need for more or different information, the sense of something important pending. The problem doesn't have to be big. The fact that it draws your attention but stays hidden shows there is something deeper at work.

Making a question out of this problem has two parts. The first is soul-searching. Search out and articulate what you think and feel about it, who is involved, what is at stake, memories, dreams, what you think it might symbolize, why you are anxious or uncertain, what kind of information you feel that you need. The answer will speak directly to these concerns. A dialogue with someone else will often help bring these things out and clarify them.

Then formulate the question as clearly as you can. Focus on yourself; you are the active person. The answer will connect to you and your concerns. The clearer you make the question, the clearer the answer will be. If you can, come to a conclusion about what you want to do. Ask 'What about doing' a specific thing. Or ask for an imaginative stance: 'What should my attitude towards X be?' You can also ask 'What is happening?' in a particular part of your life or in a particular problem. For a very important question, ask twice: 'What about doing X? what about not doing X?' The oracle will offer you an image that connects you with the spirits or unconscious forces involved, the 'seeds of future events'. It will focus on you as the doer or actor. Be open to a surprise.

How to use a hexagram

To get an answer, you have to make a hexagram, which is a figure made up of six places, counted from the bottom to the top. In each place there is an **opened** or **whole** line. Each of these lines is either **stable** or **transforming**. There are 64 of these hexagrams in the *I Ching*, made up of all the possible combinations of six opened and whole lines. Each has a name and a number. Each hexagram is also thought of as being made up of two three-line figures or trigrams. There are eight trigrams, all the possible combinations of three opened and whole lines. They also have names and meanings. You use the trigrams to help you identify your hexagram, once you have made it. The potential form of a hexagram is shown in *figure 1*.

6 [   ]   **Outer**

5 [   ]   **Trigram**

4 [   ]   _____

3 [   ]   **Inner**

2 [   ]   **Trigram**

1 [   ]   _____

Number: _____

Name: _____

Figure 1   The potential form of a hexagram

In each of these six places there can be one of four kinds of lines, a **stable yin line**, a **stable yang line**, a **transforming yang line** or a **transforming yin line** (*figure 2*). All methods of making a hexagram produce six of these lines.

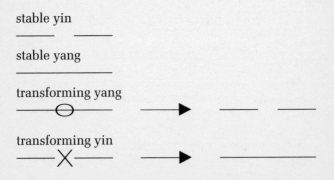

stable yin

stable yang

transforming yang

transforming yin

Figure 2   The lines used in making a hexagram

Traditionally, there are two ways to make a hexagram: by throwing 3 coins 6 times, or counting out 50 yarrow-stalks 18 times. These methods are described on page 24. The coins are quick, but the mathematical odds aren't accurate. The yarrow-stalks are more accurate, in that they more clearly reflect the qualities of the two primary powers yin and yang, but the procedure is complicated and takes up to an hour.

Making a hexagram with marbles

Recently, a new way that combines the two was invented. It is as simple and direct as the coins, but has the same mathematical odds as the yarrow-stalks. You need a small basket or large cup and a total of 16 marbles of 4 different colours: one of one colour, three of a second colour, five of a third colour and seven of a fourth colour. You can also use 16 identical sticks or stones with 4 different markings.

Each colour represents a different kind of line. First, decide and write down which colour will represent which kind of line. Then, put one marble of the first colour into the basket. This represents the least frequent line, a yin line changing into a yang line (1 out of 16 chances). Put three marbles of the second colour into the basket. They represent yang lines changing into yin lines (3 out of 16 chances). Put five marbles of the third colour into the basket. They represent stable yang lines (5 out of 16 chances). Put seven marbles of the fourth colour into the basket. They represent stable yin lines (7 out of 16 chances). These ratios reflect how yin energy likes to stay where it is, and how yang energy likes to move.

Now, shake and mix the marbles. Without looking, pick one from the basket. Draw the kind of line this colour represents at the bottom of your hexagram. Put the marble back into the basket, shake the basket again and, without looking, pick out a second marble. Draw the kind of line this colour represents in the second place of your hexagram. Replace the marble back in the basket, shake it and pick a third time, again without looking. Draw the line this colour represents in the third place of your hexagram. Now you have completed the lower or inner trigram. Put the marble back into the basket, shake it and pick a fourth time. Draw the line this colour represents in the fourth place of your hexagram. Put the marble back into the basket, shake it and pick a fifth time. Draw the kind of line this colour represents in the fifth place of your hexagram. Put the marble back into the basket, shake it, and pick a sixth and last time. Draw the kind of line this colour represents in the sixth place of your hexagram. You have now made the upper or outer trigram and completed your Primary Hexagram. If any of the lines are changing or *transforming* into their opposites, they will produce a second hexagram, the Relating Hexagram. Make this new hexagram by changing the lines that were indicated. All the other lines stay the same. You can use the form in *figure 3* to record your results.

6 [	]	**Outer**	[	]
5 [	]	**Trigram**	[	]
4 [	]	_____	[	]
3 [	]	**Inner**	[	]
2 [	]	**Trigram**	[	]
1 [	]	_____	[	]

Primary Hexagram   *transforms to:*   **Relating Hexagram**

No: ____   No: ____

Name:_____   Name:_____

Figure 3   How to record your hexagrams

Now turn to the Key to the Hexagrams on pages 26 – 27. Look at your first or Primary Hexagram. Locate the inner or lower trigram from this hexagram on the left of the chart, and the outer or upper trigram on the row above. Where these columns meet you will find the hexagram number. Write it down. Do the same for your Relating Hexagram, if you have one. Find the Divinatory Figure attached to your hexagrams, which are given in numerical order on pages 28 – 29. You should read your Primary Hexagram, and any Transforming Lines that were indicated in your consultation. Then read the first part of your Relating Hexagram, without reading any of the lines.

How the hexagrams work

We call the 64 'chapters' of the *I Ching* 'hexagrams', but this is a bit misleading. The original word refers to the divinatory figure as a whole: name, texts and linear figures. Strictly, only the six-line graph that lets you get an answer to your question is a 'hexagram'. The 64 divinatory figures are like 'piles' of things: words, ideas, images and lines. Taken all together, they suggest the active quality of the time, the 'motor' that is driving your problem.

The 64 divinatory figures appear in this book in a special way. They are all focused on 'you' as the one things are happening to, the one that needs to act. They seek to help you see into your situation and find the most effective, imaginative way to deal with it.

Imagine the answer to your question was hexagram **59 Dispersing**. The first thing to look at is the six-line hexagram figure and the *name*. The name is the basic theme for everything that is occurring. This is accompanied by the **Keywords**. These translate the theme into action and give you a basic strategy to take: *Clear away what is blocking the light*. The first part of the text gives you basic images and directions. This comes from the oldest part of the original text. It includes the divinatory formulas that indicated what was pleasing to the spirits and what sort of activities would be in accord with the time. This offers instructions on what to do and an indication of what the action you are asking about can bring. Here is the first part of **Dispersing**:

Dispersing describes your situation in terms of the possibility of eliminating misunderstandings, illusions and obstacles. The way to deal with it is to clear away what is blocking clarity and understanding. Scatter the clouds, melt the ice, dispel fear and illusions, clear up misunderstandings, eliminate suspicions. Let the fog lift and the sun shine through. This is pleasing to the spirits. Through it they will give you success, effective power and the capacity to bring the situation to maturity. Be like the king who imagines a temple full of images that unite people and connect them with greater forces. This is the right time to embark on a significant enterprise or to enter the stream of life with a purpose. Put your ideas to the trial. That brings profit and insight.

Then the name of this figure is repeated with all its possible meanings. This lets you feel the energy field you are dwelling in and all the actions it suggests. It can put things together in surprising ways. This usually includes a brief description of the elements or signs that make up the Chinese word, the ideogram.

Disperse, HUAN: Scatter clouds, break up obstacles; dispel illusions, fears and suspicions; clear things up, dissolve resistance; untie, separate; change and mobilize what is rigid; melting ice, floods, fog lifting and clearing away. The ideogram portrays water and the sign for expand. It suggests changing form through expanding or scattering.

The next section gives you the commentary texts. They include a description of the hexagram graph, further advice derived from what was called the Nuclear Hexagram, explanations, associations, philosophical ideas and an analysis of how the two basic energies are acting in this situation. It is all there to help you understand the quality of time implied by the name of your divinatory figure. Here, you can pick and choose what helps you.

The hexagram figure shows fluid movement gently penetrating the world. The wind moves above the stream. Take things in and provide what is needed. When something is expressed it scatters and spreads clarity. This is dispersing. Dispersing means that the light shines through. The early kings used this time to make offerings to the highest powers and establish temples. Dispersing pleases the spirits. Through it they will give you success, effective power and the capacity to bring the situation to maturity. What is solid and strong keeps coming without being exhausted. What is supple and flexible acquires the outer situation and connects with the strong above. Be like the king who imagines a temple full of images that connect with greater forces. This is the right time to embark on a significant enterprise or to enter the stream of life with a purpose. Make ready your vehicle, the boat that will carry you, and go on to achieve something solid.

Then come the **Transforming Lines**, traditionally indicated by the number nine for a transforming yang line or a six for a transforming yin line. These Transforming Lines combine the oldest texts and the newer commentary. They are the 'hot spots' that tell you where and how things are moving and suggest specific strategies to deal with them. You should read these texts *only* when a line in your Primary Hexagram is changing into its opposite. If you have no Transforming Lines, it indicates that there is no change visible yet in the situation you asked about. If you have more than one Transforming Line, they can indicate forces pulling you in different directions, the evolution of the situation, or the various choices that are available to you. They will be contradictory if the forces acting on you are contradictory. Within each line there is a section called *Direction*. This uses a method of analyzing related hexagrams to give you a road sign, a hint of what may be coming. This helps you focus the line texts. Here is an example from **Dispersing**. If you had a Transforming Line in the second place, you would read:

Nine at-second: Disperse the obstacles by leaving what you are leaning on. Let go of your habitual support. By doing this you will acquire what you desire. *Direction*: Let everything come into view and find the central meaning. Strip away your old ideas and be open to new ones. Provide what is needed.

This would tell you that in order to clear up your situation, you should let go of things you normally depend on. You should strip away your habitual ways of looking at the matter at hand and let all the different aspects come into view. In that way you will see the central meaning and acquire what you wish.

When this line changes, it generates the Relating Hexagram, in this case **20 Viewing**. The name of the Relating Hexagram tells you how you can relate to the answer as a whole.

Viewing describes your situation in terms of the need to look without acting in order to find the right perspective. The way to deal with it is to let everything emerge and divine the central meaning. Particularly, look at what you usually don't want to see or think about. This figure describes a particular moment in a religious ceremony, when the purification has been made and the libation is about to be poured out. Have confidence. Examining things will bring you the insight you need. When you have made the preparations, the spirit will arrive and carry you through.

This indicates the perspective you should take on the problem. It may also indicate a possible outcome, a warning, your desires or goals, depending on what and how you asked. Here, it would suggest that the actions involved are imaginative actions. Looking into the situation at hand from a new and deeper perspective will of itself bring the answer.

The words of the hexagrams will suggest many things. The divinatory formulas and directions are there to give you an idea of the general flow and to warn of pitfalls and traps. Let all these things work on you, bringing up feelings, ideas, insights. What the *I* will always try to do is to get energy moving in your situation and direct it in the most fertile and interesting way. It is interested in both protecting you and challenging you to talk with your spirits.

An explanation of yin and yang

Like all of the world's important books, people have been thinking about the *I Ching* for thousands of years. You can go on learning about it as long as you like. It is fascinating to keep a record of your questions and answers and use them to build up a net of associations, your own *I Ching* collage. But the first and most important thing the *I Ching* does is to give you advice about what you can do in a particular situation to stay in touch with *tao*, spirit or creative energy.

Yin and yang are important. They are the basic categories of most Eastern thought and are becoming a part of our culture.

Think of them as two fundamental kinds of energy that come together to make the world as we know it. Yin energy gives everything form; it makes things exist, concrete, in the here and now. Yang energy, on the other hand, is dynamic and driving. It arouses and changes things. Yin receives, yang initiates. But remember, everything is a constantly changing *mixture* of the two, and this includes women and men. Woman and man are symbols for yin and yang, but yin and yang are not symbols for women and men. Each of us is both, and the relation is constantly changing: too much yin and everything stops; too much yang and everything burns up. The aim is to be constantly adjusting the balance between the two, which brings us to something very interesting. The words yin and yang are not as old as the *I Ching*. They came later, when the old magic was codified into a science. What came first were the two kinds of lines, **opened** and **whole**, and two ways of acting called **small** and **great** or **supple** and **solid**. When the oracle perceives that your situation 'needs yin', you will be advised to act in a **small** and **supple** way: be flexible, soft, take each thing as it comes and adapt to it. When your situation 'needs yang', you will be advised to act in a **great** and **solid** way: be firm, persistent, strong, have one single idea, impose your will on things. These attitudes have nothing to do with which gender you are. Neither one is morally right; what *is* right is to use them in harmony with your own spirit and the spirit of the time.

Living with the *tao*

Nothing can tell you exactly what will happen to you, because time and fate are creative; they are continually being made. What the oracle can do is give you an image of the forces or spirits at work in your situation, and advice about how to handle it from the perspective of someone who wants to live with the *tao*. This is information you can use. It shows the direction things are moving in the imagination. It opens a dialogue with the hidden spirits. Live with the images, carry them around with you and let them open up ways of understanding and dealing with your situation. As you do this, spirit accumulates. You can feel it happening; you feel that you are connected to something, not just adrift. There is a real presence in the *I Ching's* advice. It can mobilize the deeper levels of your own spirit to help you find your way in the world. That's what an oracle does; and that is what this book is all about.

Becoming involved with your spiritual evolution

Most *I Chings* impose a very particular moral and philosophical interpretation on the divinatory images. That was true even in China, after the Neo-Confucians, and we have to go outside the ruling-class tradition to find the spirit again. This book is based on the first translation in the West to recognize and use the power of the images themselves. It gives you the kind of information a diviner would use to help you see into your situation. Though it recognizes certain things as significant, it doesn't force you into a particular moral code. That's important, in magic, in divination, in psychology and in living. The diviner doesn't say, 'I know it all', or 'I am a superior person', or 'There is only one way to do things', or 'I know the way to spiritual salvation'. What the diviner says is that it looks like these forces are evident in your situation, and these are the kind of things you can do to work with them. This gives you tools, help, a feeling of contact, clues to avoid the worst kinds of mistakes and a sense of being involved with your spiritual evolution rather than being cut off from it.

The next stage

If you have your question, and you made a hexagram, turn to the texts and read them. This is the kind of information and concern you would get if you visited a traditional diviner or soul-doctor. You will probably be shocked at how directly some of it relates to your situation. Other parts take a while to sink in. Read the answer, think about it, enjoy it, take it with you, step into it as if it were a costume or a role and see what happens. The oracle doesn't save your soul. What it does is help you imagine it.

THE EIGHT TRIGRAMS

The eight trigrams are all the possible combinations of three **opened** and **whole** lines. Thinking in terms of trigrams evolved later than the two kinds of lines and the hexagram figures. It characterizes the desire for systems and synthesis characteristic of the Han Dynasty, the period beginning about 200BCE that turned the *I* into a 'classic'. There are many associations with these trigrams. Later Chinese thinkers used them to amalgamate all the different methods of analyzing the world.

The trigrams also symbolize and invoke different kinds of spirit-energy. Each of the 64 hexagrams was seen as a combination of two of these trigrams and the spirits they represent. One of them presides over the inner world, one over the outer world. The oracle will give you a hint as to how these spirits are relating, so that you might understand what the tensions and possibilities of the moment are.

Here are the most fundamental associations:

EIGHT TRIGRAMS AND THEIR ATTRIBUTES

TRIGRAM	IMAGE	ACTION	SYMBOL
	FORCE CH'IEN	PERSISTING	HEAVEN
	FIELD K'UN	YIELDING	EARTH
	SHAKE CHEN	STIRRING-UP	THUNDER
	GORGE K'AN	VENTURING FALLING	STREAM
	BOUND KEN	STOPPING	MOUNTAIN
	GROUND SUN	ENTERING	WOOD WIND
	RADIANCE LI	CONGREGATING	FIRE BRIGHTNESS
	OPEN TUI	STIMULATING	MIST

THE CONCEPTUAL ORDER ACCORDING TO FU HSI

FORCE/FIELD	SHAKE/GROUND	GORGE/RADIANCE	BOUND/OPEN

☰ **Force,** CH'IEN: Force is a dragon, a creative spirit power that lives in the waters and in the heavens. This spirit is a dynamic shape-changer. It can give you creative power and the strength to endure, to persist in time. There is a quality of struggle associated with Force, a struggle to grapple with primary powers. It is reflected in the way opposing forces grapple together to form the basis of the world around us. It was associated with heaven, the sovereign, and the father. It is made of only whole lines.

☷ **Field,** K'UN: Field is the womb that gives birth to all things. This spirit nourishes everything; without it nothing could exist. It can give you the power to give shape to things, to make thoughts and images visible. This is reflected in the way the earth yields and serves. It yields to an impulse in order to yield a harvest. There is a quality of labour associated with Field, work undertaken together, like sowing and harvesting a crop. It was associated with earth (as beneath heaven), the mother, and the minister or courtier. It is made up of only opened lines.

☳ **Shake,** CHEN: Shake is the frightening and inspiring thunder spirit, who bursts forth from the earth below to arouse, excite and disturb things. This spirit stirs things up and brings them out of hiding, like plants bursting forth from the earth in the spring. It can arouse your dormant energy through a shock, and give you the strength to undertake and move heavy things. Shake is a warrior spirit, an energetic and protective force. It was associated with the first or eldest son, who began the new generation and provided for the parents and ancestors. You can see it as the stirring whole line that emerges below two dormant opened lines.

☴ **Ground,** SUN: Ground is the gently penetrating and nourishing spirit of wood and wind. It is a subtle, beautiful and gentle spirit that permeates things and brings them to maturity. Ground presides over mating, coupling and marriages, creating and spreading new seeds. You can see this spirit in the way trees grow, slowly permeating the earth and air around them, and in the way moving air permeates and creates an 'atmosphere' that influences how you think and feel. Ground can give you the ability to establish and nourish things. It was associated with the first or eldest daughter, who is given in marriage and presides over the new house. You can see it as the opened line that nourishes two whole lines from below, subtly penetrating and influencing them.

21

☵ **Gorge**, K'AN: Gorge is the impetuous and adventurous spirit of water flowing in rivers and streams. Gorge takes risks, like water falling, filling the holes in its path and flowing on. There is a quality of difficult but worthwhile labour associated with Gorge. It dissolves things, carries them forward and cannot be stopped. This spirit can give you the energy to take risks, to focus your energy at a critical point, to confront and overcome obstacles. It was associated with the middle son, courageous and venturesome, who must take chances, leave the house, or establish a new concern. You can see it as the single whole line between two constraining opened lines, flowing on without hesitation or reserve.

☲ **Radiance**, LI: Radiance is the spirit of fire, light and warmth, the hearth fire, the sun and the heavenly bodies, and the magical power of awareness. It spreads light in all directions, warming and illuminating, a shape-changing bird with brilliant plumage that comes to rest on things. Radiance clings together with what it illuminates, warming it and making it visible. It can give you the power to see and understand things, and to articulate ideas and goals. It was associated with the middle daughter, mature, supportive, and dependent. You can see it as the single opened line that holds two whole lines together, uniting and illuminating them.

☶ **Bound**, KEN: Bound is the mountain spirit, who fixes limits and brings things to a close. Bound encloses and marks things off. It is the end that prepares a new beginning. This spirit suggests the Palace of the Immortals, the eternal images that end and begin all things. It can give you the power to articulate what you have gone through and make your accomplishments clear. It was associated with the youngest son, the limit and end of the family. You can see it as the single whole line that stops two opened lines beneath it.

☱ **Open**, TUI: Open is the spirit of water accumulating and spreading. It is the vapors that rise from lakes, ponds and marshes that stimulate, fertilize and enrich. The friendliest and most joyous of spirits, Open is a place to gather together. It brings stimulating words, profitable exchange, responsive, free and cheerful interaction, freedom from constraint. It is the feeling that comes when the harvest has been gathered and you are sure of the winter ahead. Open can give you persuasive and inspiring speech, the ability to rouse things to action and create good feeling. It also sponsors magic, the words that can invoke spirits, help humans and change the way we see things. It was associated with the youngest daughter, light-hearted, whimsical and magical. You can see it in the single opened line that leads two whole lines forward.

COINS AND YARROW-STALKS

There are two traditional ways of consulting the *I Ching*. One uses three coins, the other a set of 50 yarrow-stalks (*achillea millfolium*). Each of these methods produces one of four numbers (6, 7, 8 or 9) six times. These six numbers produce the six lines of the hexagram.

The coin oracle was popularized in the Southern Sung period (1127 – 1279) and has been used for several hundred years. It yields quick results. But it has a bias, for the odds are symmetrical. This reflects a binary choice between yin and yang. It does not penetrate as deeply into the situation as the yarrow-stalk oracle with its asymmetrical relation of the two primary powers.

To use the coin oracle, you must have three similar coins. Heads are yang and have the value 3. Tails are yin and have the value 2. Throw the coins six times and add up the numbers each time. For each throw record the number and the kind of line it refers to (6 = transforming yin; 7 = stable yang; 8 = stable yin; 9 = transforming yang). Form your hexagram from the bottom up, then use the Key to the Hexagrams on pages 26 – 27 to determine its number and name.

To use the older and more traditional yarrow-stalk oracle, you need a set of 50 thin sticks about 12 – 16 in long, traditionally yarrow or *achillea millfolium*, taken from the tips of the plants. The basic unit of this process is dividing and counting out the bunch of yarrow-stalks six times. Each time this is done it produces a number and thus a line of your hexagram.

- Put the bunch of 50 yarrow-stalks on the table in front of you. Take one stalk and put it aside. This is the Observer or Witness. It will remain unused *through the entire process of forming a hexagram*.
- Divide the remaining bunch into two random portions.
- Take one stalk from the pile on your left. Put it between the fourth and fifth fingers of your left hand.
- Pick the pile on the right up in your left hand, and count it out with your right hand in groups of four, laying them out clearly on the table. Count out the sticks until you have a remainder of 4, 3, 2, or 1. You must have a remainder.
- Put this remainder between the third and fourth fingers of your left hand.
- Take the remaining pile and count it out in groups of four, until you have a remainder of 4, 3, 2, or 1. Lay the groups out clearly on the table. Put the remainder between the second and third fingers of your left hand.
- Take all the stalks from between your fingers and lay them aside. They are out *for this round*.
- Make one bunch of the stalks that remain and repeat the procedure. Again, put the stalks between your fingers at the end of the process aside.
- Repeat the process a third time. This time, count the number of groups of four left on the table in front of you. This number should be 6, 7, 8, or 9. It indicates the first or *bottom* line of your hexagram.
- To get your hexagram, repeat this process five more times, building the hexagram from the bottom up. When you finish, gather the stalks and return them to their container or wrapping. Then use the Key to the Hexagrams on pages 26 – 27 to find the hexagram numbers.

KEY TO THE HEXAGRAMS

To find the hexagram that the Oracle has given you as an answer to your question, locate the lower trigram on the left and the upper trigram on the top of the chart . Then turn to the hexagram text that the number indicates.

UPPER TRIGRAMS

LOWER TRIGRAMS	FORCE	FIELD	SHAKE	GORGE
FORCE	1	11	34	5
FIELD	12	2	16	8
SHAKE	25	24	51	3
GORGE	6	7	40	29
BOUND	33	15	62	39
GROUND	44	46	32	48
RADIANCE	13	36	55	63
OPEN	10	19	54	60

UPPER TRIGRAMS

LOWER TRIGRAMS

BOUND	GROUND	RADIANCE	OPEN	
26	9	14	43	FORCE
23	20	35	45	FIELD
27	42	21	17	SHAKE
4	59	64	47	GORGE
52	53	56	31	BOUND
18	57	50	28	GROUND
22	37	30	49	RADIANCE
41	61	38	58	OPEN

The Hexagrams by Number and Name

THE 64 DIVINATORY FIGURES

1 Force / Persisting,
CH'IEN

**Keywords: Persist and create.
Make your efforts enduring.**

Force describes your situation in terms of the primal power of spirit to create and destroy. Its symbols are the inspiring power of heaven, the light of the sun that causes everything to grow, the fertilizing rain and the creative energy of the dragon that breaks through boundaries. You are confronted with many obstacles. The way to deal with them is to persist, for you are in contact with fundamental creative energy. Take action. Be dynamic, strong, untiring, tenacious and enduring. Continue on your path and don't be dismayed. Ride the power of the dragon and bring the fertilizing rain. Your situation contains great creative potential. It can open up a whole new cycle of time.

Force/Persisting, CH'IEN: Spirit power, creative energy; forward motion; dynamic, enduring; firm, stable; activate, inspire; heaven, masculine, ruler; exhaust, destroy, dry up, clear away; *also:* Strong, robust, tenacious, untiring. The ideogram portrays moving energy, the sun and growing plants.

The hexagram figure shows creative force in action. Heaven moves and persists. This spirit power is available to you. Use it as a source of strength and determination in order to continue on without pause. This great force is the beginning of things. As the clouds spread and the rain falls, all things flow into their shapes. It shows you the end that brings a new beginning, the way energy moves in the world and the proper time to accomplish something. If you become aware of its movement, you can ride this energy in its six different shapes as if it were six dragons. The way of force is to change and transform things. It makes the innate spirit within each being manifest. This protects the great harmony of the world. Take advantage of it. Use this creative energy to produce ideas that inspire people and give them models of transformation. Bring together what belongs together. What you create can be the source of a deep and self-renewing peace of mind.

Transforming Lines

Initial nine: The dragon, your creative power, is immersed in the waters below. It's already working, though hidden and secret. Don't try to use it yet. *Direction:* Have no doubts. You are coupled with a creative force.

Nine at-second: The dragon, your creative power, appears in a field of activity. Your ability to realize things is spreading. See great people who can help you. Let your idea permeate and organize things. *Direction:* Bring people together. Give them a goal. You are coupled with a creative force.

Nine at-third: If you want to stay in touch with the *tao,* this is a time of incessant activity. Creative energy is doubled. You are active all day long. As night falls, it finds you fearful and cautious. A major change is going on. It looks dangerous, as if you are confronting an angry old ghost. You are not making a mistake. Turn your back on what you used to do. Your world may seem upside down, but it is actually the return of the *tao*. *Direction:* Make your own way step by step. Find a supportive group. Stay inside it. Gather energy for a decisive new move.

Nine at-fourth: You make no mistake by playing. Dance in deep waters with ease. Your playfulness can puncture the ponderous. Don't get nailed down. Your creative energy is most certainly advancing. *Direction:* Accumulate small things to build up something great. Turn potential conflict into creative tension. The situation is already changing.

Nine at-fifth: Your dragon is flying in the heavens. Spread your wings. Your creative energy has found a visible field of activity. See great people who can help you. Let your central idea permeate and influence everything around you. Make things, build things, create and establish. *Direction:* This begins a rich and fertile time, spreading warmth and light. Be resolute. You are connected with a creative force.

Nine above: There is a difference between creative force and being overbearing. Avoid arrogance. Avoid scorn and disparaging others. If you try to enforce your authority through a display of force, you will most certainly have cause to regret it. This is too much. It can't last. *Direction:* Resolve to do better.

All nines: A group of dragons without a leader, their creative energies co-operating. Don't try to impose a focus. Take a secondary position. This generates meaning and good fortune by releasing transformative energy. The inherent power of the spirit is blocking the emergence of a leader. Accept it and change your ideas. *Direction:* Don't take the lead. Be open to the new. Provide what is needed.

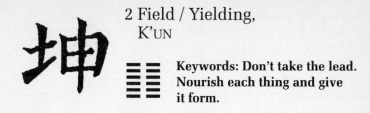

2 Field / Yielding, K'UN

Keywords: Don't take the lead. Nourish each thing and give it form.

Field describes your situation in terms of the primal power to nourish and give things form. Its symbols are the earth, the moon, the mother, the devoted servant, the mare. You are confronted with many conflicting forces. The way to deal with them is to yield to each thing, nourishing it and providing what it needs to exist. You are in contact with the fundamental power to give things form. This will yield results. It will open up a whole new cycle of time. At first you will be confused by the profusion of things. Keep your sense of purpose. Do whatever presents itself to be done without judging it. This brings profit and insight. You can acquire what you desire and achieve mastery. Join with others in concrete projects, but don't shirk your own responsibility. Put your ideas to the trial. Remain calm and assured. Don't take the lead. This generates meaning and good fortune by releasing transformative energy.

> **Field/Yielding,** K'UN: The visible surface of the world; concrete existence, the fundamental power to give things form; earth, moon, mother, wife, servants, ministers; supple strength, receptive power; welcome, consent to, respond to an appeal; *also:* Yield, give birth, bear fruit; agree, follow, obey; nourish, provide, serve, work for, work with. The ideogram portrays the spirits of the earth.

The hexagram figure shows an enduring power to yield and serve. The potency of earth. Let your power to realize things be so generous that it carries everything that approaches you. Field gives birth. It yields and receives. Its power to accept and give things form is unlimited. Reflect this through your generosity. Cherish each thing so its essential quality shines through. Accept it and help it grow. Identify yourself with the earth. Be fertile and tireless. Move without drawing boundaries. Use the oracle to stay in touch with the *tao*. At first you will be confused and let go of the way. Don't be worried by your confusion. Through yielding sincerely to each thing, you will acquire a new set of rules. Join with people on concrete projects. That can help you sort things out. Let your partners go when you are ready to bring things to completion. That will bring you rewards. Put your ideas to the trial. Remain calm and quiet. Accept hidden processes and energies. Don't define things by setting up boundaries.

Transforming Lines

Initial six: If you tread on the frost, you will harden the ice. Act slowly, carefully, and persistently to establish a durable base. *Direction:* This is the return of something important. Be open to it. Don't take the lead. Provide what is needed.

Six at-second: You can establish something solid now with ease. Proceed directly and sincerely to lay it out. Reform, clarify, correct the crooked. Focus on a single central idea. You don't need to repeat yourself or rehearse anything. Go right to the point. Stir things up. There is nothing for which this will not, ultimately, be advantageous. The way of the earth shines through it. *Direction:* Organize your forces. This is the return of something important. Be open to it. Provide what is needed.

Six at-third: Act through a design that contains and conceals. This is the place of hidden excellence. You may be engaged in serious activities. Don't bring your part in them to an end through a need to be seen. Send out feelers in new directions. Through them you can be greatly enlightened. *Direction:* Keep your words clear and close to the facts. Release bound energy. The situation is already changing.

Six at-fourth: Bundled in a bag, enclosed and enveloped. This idea is pregnant with possibilities. There is nothing to praise or blame. What you desire is already there. Careful consideration won't do you any harm. *Direction:* Provide reserves of strength for the future. Re-imagine the situation. Gather energy for a decisive new move.

Six at-fifth: A yellow ceremonial garment covers your lower body. Accept hidden processes. What is happening may be confusing, but it will be the source of great good fortune and meaningful events. Have patience. Accept hidden processes. What is going on will affect you deeply and positively. *Direction:* Change who you associate with. Strip away your old ideas. Be open to new ones. Provide what is needed.

Six above: The dragons are fighting, sky powers and earth powers. You can see them out beyond the city walls, where their blood is flowing. They are exhausting themselves in a needless struggle for supremacy. If you are responsible, yield, give way, restore peace. If you are not, stay low and get out of the way. *Direction:* Strip away your old ideas. Be open to new ones. Provide what is needed.

All sixes: This is a long-term effort from which great benefits will flow. To keep things in motion, use the oracle and its power of transformation often. Use a single central idea to bring things to completion. *Direction:* Take action.

3 Sprouting,
Chun

Keywords: Help everything find the right place to grow.

Sprouting describes your situation in terms of beginning growth. The way to deal with it is to assemble things and accumulate energy for a difficult yet exciting task. Like young plants breaking through the covering earth, this will open an entire new cycle of time. Don't try to impose your ideas or direct things. There are many new possibilities emerging. Take advantage of them by installing helpers and delegating responsibilities. Stake out your territory, establish bases of operation, assemble the troops, collect your possessions. That brings profit and insight.

Sprout, CHUN: Begin or cause to grow; assemble, accumulate, amass, hoard; establish a base of operations, establish troops at the borders; difficult, painful, arduous; the difficulties at the beginning of an endeavour. The ideogram portrays a young plant breaking through the crust of the earth.

The hexagram figure shows arousing new energy confronting unknown risks. Clouds and thunder. Strip away old ideas. Abundant new possibilities are being born. Stay where you are and let everything come into view. Set up structures and ideas that can weave things together. This is a stirring time. It releases many new possibilities. There is heavy work to be done. Things are full to overflowing. The atmosphere is the dusky light before daybreak. Things are coming at you from all sides. Don't try to soothe and pacify them. Install your helpers and give everything a place. This chaotic profusion is in accord with the time. It is the beginning of a new world.

Transforming Lines

Initial nine: A large rock and a grave post. Establish stable foundations that are rooted in the past. Go on with your efforts and empower people to help you. Your purpose is moving correctly. Look at what you normally think is beneath you. You will find an undeveloped potential that can give you great support. *Direction:* Change who you are associating with. Strip away old ideas. Don't take the lead. Provide what is needed.

Six at-second: Every time you start something, you run into obstacles and are unable to advance. You are mounted on your horse, all your virtues displayed, yet you are standing still. Don't lose courage. The things that are frustrating you are not out to harm you, no matter how bad it may seem. Don't use force. Try to negotiate alliances, even though such a marriage will take a long time to bear fruit. This is heavy going, but stick with it. In the long run the whole situation will be reversed. There are active forces involved that are beyond your control. *Direction:* Articulate your needs and desires. Take things in. Provide what is needed.

Six at-third: You don't really know what you are doing. Stop. If you go on this way, you will find yourself lost in a trackless forest and what you are hunting for will vanish. Someone who uses the oracle to stay in touch with the *tao* would stop at the first sign. Spare yourself shame, regret and exhaustion. Listen to this advice. *Direction:* The situation is already changing.

Six at-fourth: You are mounted on your horse, all your virtues displayed, yet you are standing still. Don't use force to end your frustration. Seek alliances and marriages. There is nothing for which this will not, ultimately, be advantageous. Keep going. Actively pursue what you need. This will generate meaning and good fortune by releasing transformative energy. You can achieve renown and new awareness. *Direction:* Follow the natural course of events. Proceed step by step. Gather energy for a decisive new move.

Nine at-fifth: You have found the fertile juice, the genius, the source of wealth. This will generate meaning and good fortune if you can adapt it to each thing that needs it. If you insist on imposing your ideas, you will be cut off from the spirits and left open to danger. Spread it out, give everyone what they need. Things aren't clear enough yet. *Direction:* This is the return of something important. Be open to it. Don't take the lead. Provide what is needed.

Six above: Mounted on your horse, all your virtues displayed, yet you are standing still. This situation is bleeding you to death. Why let it go on any further? *Direction:* A better time is coming. Strip away old ideas and be open to new ones. Provide what is needed.

4 Enveloping,
MENG

Keywords: Don't act. You are unaware. Protect the hidden growth.

Enveloping describes your situation in terms of staying under cover. You are immature and your awareness of the problem is dull and clouded. The way to deal with it is to accept being hidden in order to nurture growing awareness. Pull the covers over. Put the lid on. There is much concealed from you. You don't really know what you are doing. But the beginnings are definitely there, even if you can't yet see them. You didn't ask for this problem. It asked for you and it belongs with you. The first time you consult the oracle about this, it will advise and inform you. If you keep on asking, you muddy the waters. Your awareness must grow and change. Put your ideas to the trial. That brings profit and insight. Keep working on your problem. It will educate you.

> **Envelop,** MENG: Cover, hide, conceal; lid, covering; dull, unaware, ignorant; uneducated; young, undeveloped, fragile; unseen beginnings; *also:* A parasitic and magical plant. The ideogram portrays a plant and a cover. It suggests nurturing hidden growth.

The hexagram figure shows an outer obstacle that protects an inner source. Below the mountain a spring emerges. Energy is returning below. Turn back to meet it. The answer is already there, but it is immature and has to be protected. Enveloping means being immature. Don't pretend you know it already. Accept being visibly confused. Work on things gradually, like a plant bearing fruit. Aggressive action is blocked because this is the season for inner growth. The oracle confirms this. Don't keep asking the same question. Use your confusion to envelop your premature desire to act. What you see as an obstacle is there to nourish your awareness and correct your one-sided view of things. When you can really accept and understand this, you will most certainly become wise.

Transforming Lines

Initial six: Correct the way you use enveloping. To restrain real wrongdoers brings profit and insight. But you have lost the right track. You have shackled something that you should stimulate and set free. Adjust this balance. Free and redirect the energy you need to go forward. *Direction:* Decrease your present involvements. Something significant is returning. Be open to it. Don't take the lead. Provide what is needed.

Nine at-second: Turn enveloping into caring and being responsible. This generates meaning and good fortune by releasing transformative energy. Take a wife, support a household. Articulate relations within the dwelling place. *Direction:* Strip away your old ideas. Be open to the new. Provide what is needed.

Six at-third: Don't try to grasp what you want. Don't make or deal in idealized images of power or satisfaction. You will lose your independence and the power to express yourself. There is nothing of value to be gained by acting this way. *Direction:* The situation is corrupt. If you let yourself be led out of it, you will realize a hidden potential. The situation is already changing.

Six at-fourth: Enveloping has turned to confining. Your solitary isolation is distancing you from the real substance of things. Correct your thinking and return to the way. *Direction:* Gather energy for a decisive new move.

Six at-fifth: You are young and your awareness is enveloped. Accept it. This generates meaning and good fortune by releasing transformative energy. Yield and work with the situation. Gently penetrate to the core. *Direction:* Disperse obstacles to understanding. Take things in. Don't try to lead. Be open to the new.

Nine above: This conflict is of your own making. You are attacking what envelops you, so it, in turn, attacks you. Resist the temptation to break rules and behave violently. By yielding and working with the situation, you can connect what is above and below. *Direction:* Organize yourself. Something significant is returning. Be open to it. Don't take the lead. Provide what is needed.

5 Attending, Hsü

Keywords: Wait for the right time. Attend to what is needed.

Attending describes your situation in terms of waiting for and serving something. The way to deal with it is to find out what is needed and carefully wait for the right moment to act. You aren't in control of things, but in time you can provide what is needed. Act this way with confidence. You are connected to the spirits and they will carry you through. One day you will bring the rain. Look after things. Think about what is necessary. Illuminate the situation through repeated efforts. This is pleasing to the spirits. Through it they will give you success, effective power and the capacity to bring the situation to maturity. Put your ideas to the trial. That generates meaning and good fortune by releasing transformative energy. This is the right time to enter the stream of life with a goal or embark on a significant enterprise. That brings profit and insight.

Attend, Hsü: Take care of, look out for, serve; necessary, need, call for; provide what is needed; wait for, hesitate, doubt; stopped by rain; know how to wait, have patience and focus. The ideogram portrays rain and a sign that means both stop and source. It suggests being forced to wait and the ability to bring rain.

The hexagram figure shows an inner force confronting outer danger. Clouds mounting above heaven. Turn potential conflict into creative tension. Attend wholeheartedly to the needs at hand. There is something immature in your situation that must be nourished. Eating and drinking together are in harmony with the *tao*. They serve to nourish the spirits. This isn't a time to advance yourself, to champion a cause or climb a mountain. Spread repose and delight. Help leisure, peace of mind, pleasure and harmony permeate the situation like a banquet or feast. Have patience. Carefully yield to precedence and persist in your efforts. Don't think of your waiting and care as an exhausting burden. It is how you can act justly and righteously in this situation and connect what you are doing with the spirit above. It will bring you accomplishment and praise.

Transforming Lines

Initial nine: Attending at the frontier between the country and the city. This is heavy going. Persevere. Don't oppose the movement. It will bring you profit and insight. You haven't let go of your fundamental principles. *Direction:* Stay connected to the source of your values. Turn potential conflict into creative tension. The situation is already changing.

Nine at-second: Attending on the sands, the shore laid bare by receding water. Small people and small talk surround you. Adapt to it. The source of all this is located in the centre, which is where you want to go. Going through with your plans will generate meaning and good fortune by releasing transformative energy. *Direction:* The situation is already changing.

Nine at-third: You are headed for the bogs, where you will be mired down and unable to move. This affair will end in disaster. Think about it. The calamity hasn't reached you yet. If you don't wish to be surrounded by outlaws, give it some serious consideration. Perhaps you can avoid destruction if you understand what you did to create this situation. *Direction:* Set limits. Take things in. Be open to new ideas.

Six at-fourth: Whatever you think you are waiting for, what you are headed for is blood. You are stuck in a cave, a pit that may end up as a grave. Stir yourself up. You can be saved if you listen. *Direction:* Be resolute. Take action. You are connected to a creative force.

Nine at-fifth: Attend to taking in spirits. Join with others in eating, drinking and being filled with spirit. This corrects one-sidedness and isolation. Putting your ideas to the trial generates meaning and good fortune by releasing transformative energy. This spirit separates what is worthy from what is unworthy. *Direction:* A fertile and prosperous time is coming. If you let yourself be led, you can realize a hidden potential. The situation is already changing.

Six above: Enter the cave, the enclosed place. You will soon have visitors, even though you have not urged them to come. Three people are on their way. Respect them. They will help you out of an inappropriate situation. You can gain something important by doing so. *Direction:* Accumulate small things to achieve something great. Turn potential conflict into creative tension. The situation is already changing.

6 Arguing,
Sung

**Keywords: Argue your position.
Don't act on it.**

Arguing describes your situation in terms of a dispute. The way to deal with it is to clarify and actively express your viewpoint without trying to escalate the conflict. Act this way with confidence. You are linked to the spirits and they will carry you through. Dispute things. Present your case. Plead in court. Demand justice. Don't be afraid or intimidated. Restrain your respect and your fear of authority. Don't give in, but don't exaggerate or get involved in petty wrangles. Staying in the centre will generate meaning and good fortune by releasing transformative energy. It is advantageous to see great people. Visit those who are important and can give you advice. Try to become aware of the real purpose behind your desire. This will bring profit and insight. Don't try to bring your plans to completion. You would be cut off from the spirits and left

open to danger. It is not the right time to embark on a significant enterprise or enter the stream of life with a purpose.

> **Argue,** SUNG: Dispute, plead your case, demand justice,
> contend in front of the ruler or judge; lodge a complaint,
> begin litigation; quarrels, wrangles, controversy; correct,
> reprimand, arrive at a judgement, resolve a conflict. The
> ideogram portrays words and the sign for an official. It
> suggests pleading in front of authority.

The hexagram figure shows a struggle that lacks a solid base
for action. Heaven combined with stream contradicts movement. Something new is being prepared. Stay inside your
group. When many people eat and drink together, arguing will
break out. This is not a harmonious time. It is full of people
and ideas contradicting each other. Don't try to be helpful and
connect all these things. Use the contradictions to stimulate
and stir things up in order to plan the beginning of new activities. Go on arguing and see what it reveals. You are connected
to the spirits and they will carry you through. Don't be afraid.
By staying in the centre you will encounter what is strong and
solid. Don't try to bring your plans to completion. The time is
against it. Seeing great people brings profit and insight. It will
help you clarify your own idea. Don't try to accomplish anything concrete. Embarking on a significant enterprise now
would be like jumping into an abyss. The great stream of life
would become a whirlpool that drowns you.

Transforming Lines

Initial six: Get out of this affair. Say whatever you need to say,
complete the transaction and get free. Being clear about this
can avoid a long and bitter conflict. *Direction:* Go your way
carefully and cautiously. Find a supportive group. Stay inside
it. Gather energy for a decisive new move.

Nine at-second: Don't try to control this situation by arguing.
Change your goals and ideas and get out now. Go back to the
place where people's doors are open to you, even if you have

to skulk away. This is not a mistake. Stay below with your origins while the argument rages above you. When the distress comes to an end, you can reap the rewards of your timely return to yourself. *Direction:* Communication is blocked. You are connected to the wrong people. Proceed step by step. Gather energy for a decisive new move.

Six at-third: Take in the power to realize things that comes from your predecessors. You are confronting a dangerous situation. An angry old ghost has returned to seek revenge for past mistreatment. Confront the difficulty. Go through with your plans. This generates meaning and good fortune by releasing transformative energy. If you have a mission from a superior, you will not be able to accomplish it. Hold on to what you think is important. *Direction:* This is a fated encounter. It connects you with a creative force.

Nine at-fourth: Don't try to control this situation by arguing. Quietly and unobtrusively turn away from what you were doing. This is a mandate from fate. Something important is returning. Go to meet it. This will generate meaning and good fortune by releasing transformative energy. Don't let go of the chance. *Direction:* Clear up the misunderstandings that hold you back. Take things in. Don't take the lead. Be open to new ideas. Provide what is needed.

Nine at-fifth: Present yourself and your case with confidence and expect positive results. This is the source of great good fortune and meaningful events. Make correcting the situation your central concern. *Direction:* Gather your energy for a decisive new move.

Nine above: Perhaps you think money and position will be bestowed upon you through arguing. Think again. By the end of the morning you will be deprived of it three times over. You think you can profitably use your arguments to make people submit to you. Think again. This isn't worthy of you. It brings you no respect at all. *Direction:* Break out of isolation. Find a supportive group. Stay inside it. Gather energy for a decisive new move.

7 Legions / Leading,
SHIH

**Keywords: Organize confusion.
Then take the lead.**

Legions/Leading describes your situation in terms of organizing a confused heap of things into functional units so you can take effective action. The way to deal with it is to organize yourself and put yourself in order. Develop the capacity to lead. Look at the people you respect, and use them as models. Find who and what you need. This generates meaning and good fortune by releasing transformative energy. The ideal of this army is not just to fight. It brings order, and protects people who cannot protect themselves. It founds cities and defends what is necessary for people to live their lives. It is not a mistake to use force in this way.

Legions/Leading, SHIH: Troops, an army; leader, general, master of arms, master of a craft; organize, make functional, mobilize, discipline; take as a model, imitate. The ideogram portrays people moving around a centre.

The hexagram figure shows serving through an inner willingness to take risks. In the middle of the earth there is the stream. Something significant is returning. Be open to it. You are surrounded by a confused crowd of things, all arguing with each other. This is not a pleasant situation. It will take concern and care to correct it. Try to give each thing its proper place. Support and sustain what is beneath or outside your normal value structure. It contains a great undeveloped potential you can accumulate and nourish. Find what you need by taking risks and confronting obstacles through a desire to serve. Don't simply impose your will. This activates a central ruling principle that people will spontaneously adhere to. It generates meaning and good fortune by releasing transformative energy. It is exactly what is needed in the present situation. How could it be a mistake?

Transforming Lines

Initial six: The legions issue forth using rules and laws. Make sure these codes of right and wrong don't block essential force. Letting go of regulations cuts you off from the spirits, but so does letting the rules get in the way of what is really needed. *Direction:* A stimulating encounter is approaching. Something important returns. Be open to it. Provide what is needed.

Nine at-second: Find and stay in the centre of the legions. This is the effective leader's position, in the middle of the troops. This generates meaning and good fortune by releasing transformative energy. The powers above have given you a mandate. You receive tasks and orders that can change your life. *Direction:* Be open to new ideas. Provide what is needed.

Six at-third: Perhaps the legions you have organized are collecting dead bodies. Whether these are old memories, useless ideas, or false images of what you are doing, get rid of them. They will cut you off from the spirits and leave you open to danger. *Direction:* Make the effort. If you let yourself be led, you can realize a hidden potential. The situation is already changing.

Six at-fourth: The legions go the way of peace. This is not a mistake. You haven't let go of the rules. *Direction:* Release bound energy. The situation is already changing.

Six at-fifth: The fields are full of things you want to catch. Be careful about what you say, how and when you say it. Lead the legions into action as if you were the oldest son, the one to whom others defer. Get rid of old memories and false ideas. Don't act as if you were the younger son who was told to collect the bodies. This will cut you off from the spirits and leave you open to danger. Acting for someone else is not appropriate here, nor is telling someone else to do your work for you. *Direction:* Go for it. Take risks. Provide what is needed. Be open to new ideas.

Six above: A great leader has a mandate from the powers above. This is a time to succeed through enacting your ideas. Found cities, where people gather, and distribute the dwellings they live in. Don't be flexible and adapt to whatever crosses your path. You are in the correct position to achieve something significant. This will necessarily upset the way power and responsibility are distributed. Don't worry about it. Do what you have to do. *Direction:* The situation contains possibilities you are not yet aware of. Something important is returning. Be open to it. Provide what is needed.

8 Grouping, PI

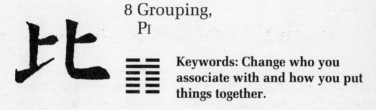

Keywords: Change who you associate with and how you put things together.

Grouping describes your situation in terms of the people and things with whom your spirit connects you. The way to deal with it is to look at who you group yourself with, and how you use ideas to categorize things. The way you put things and people together is changing. Stop and take a look around. Try to perceive essential qualities in order to get to the heart of the matter. Compare things and sort them out. Find what you belong with. You can ask your question in many different ways. The oracle will help you. This is not a mistake. It generates meaning and good fortune by releasing transformative energy. This is not a soothing time. Things are coming at you from all sides, demanding that you consider them. Do it now. If you put it off and try to manage it later, you will be cut off from the spirits and left open to danger.

> **Group,** PI: Join together, ally yourself with; find a new centre; order things in classes, compare and select; find what you belong with; harmonize, unite; neighbours; equal, identical; work together, work towards. The ideogram portrays a person who stops walking and looks around to examine things.

The hexagram figure shows relationships dissolving. The stream is above the earth. Strip away your old ideas. You are confronted with crowds of things and must find new ways to group them. This doesn't have to be painful. You can take delight in this activity. Let harmony, pleasure and elegance be a key. The early kings used this time to establish cities that connect and define the different peoples. Give each thing a place where it can actively and joyously join with others of its kind. Pay attention to what supports you from below. Try to connect your ideals and goals with an underlying support. Take advantage of the profusion of things coming at you and change now. If you put it off and try to manage it later, you will be cut off from the spirits and left open to danger.

Transforming Lines

Initial six: Have confidence in how you are grouped and who you are grouped with. You are linked to the spirits and they will carry you through. This is not a mistake. Pour in even more energy and effort, overfill the jar. Coming events will generate even more meaning and good fortune by releasing transformative energy. *Direction:* Give everything a place to grow. Strip away old ideas. Be open to new ones. Don't take the lead. Provide what is needed.

Six at-second: You are inside the group, close to the source. Let it move you. Don't let the connection slip through your fingers. Putting your ideas to the trial generates meaning and good fortune by releasing transformative energy. *Direction:* Commit yourself. Take risks. Be open to new ideas. Don't take the lead. Provide what is needed.

Six at-third: This is the wrong group for you. You are associating with the wrong people. Be careful. Think about the situation impersonally. Try to reach a place where you can avoid humiliation, grief and injury. *Direction:* Re-imagine the situation. Gather energy for a decisive new move.

Six at-fourth: You are outside the group. Use your position to your own advantage. Putting your ideas to the trial generates meaning and good fortune by releasing transformative energy. You are in this position because of your moral and intellectual worth. Stick with your work and your values. *Direction:* Assemble things for a great project. Proceed step by step. Gather energy for a decisive new move.

Nine at-fifth: If you want to enact your desires, be like the king going hunting. Don't close all the avenues of escape. This leaves the game a chance to get away, so what is caught has chosen to be with you. Don't scold people and try to make them obey you. Let go of your predatory attitudes. Let them simply fly away. You don't have to assert yourself by opposing things. Yielding and serving bring results. What you want to do is correctly centred and connected with what is above. *Direction:* Accept whatever approaches. Don't take the lead. Provide what is needed.

Six above: This is a group without a head, without a leader or an idea to inspire it. It offers you no place to complete what you want to do. Leave now or face disaster. *Direction:* Take a deeper look. Strip away old ideas and be open to new ones. Provide what is needed.

9 Small Accumulating,
HSIAO CH'U

Keywords: Accumulate small things to make something great.

Small Accumulating describes your situation in terms of confronting a great variety of things that don't seem to be related. The way to deal with it is to adapt to each thing that crosses your path in order to accumulate something great. Take the long view. Gather, herd together, retain and hoard all the little things that might seem unimportant. Think of yourself as raising animals, growing crops or bringing up children. Be flexible and adaptable. Tolerate and nourish things. The rain hasn't come yet, but the dense clouds that bring it are rolling in from the western frontier. The successful completion of your efforts is not far away.

Small, HSIAO: Little, common, unimportant; adapt to what crosses your path; take in, make smaller; dwindle, lessen; little, slim, slight; yin energy.

Accumulate, CH'U: Gather, collect, take in, hoard, retain; control, restrain; take care of, support, tolerate; tame, train or pasture animals; raise, bring up, domesticate; be tamed or controlled by something. The ideogram portrays the fertile black soil of a river delta.

The hexagram figure shows an enduring force accumulated through gentle penetration. Wind moves above heaven. Turn potential conflicts into creative tension. You need a place to accumulate things, because right now you only have a few. Focus on the inherent beauty of each thing in order to realize its potency. Above all, be flexible and adaptable. Persist in your efforts through gentle penetration and you will acquire a solid centre from which to move. The rain has not yet come. Praise and let go of what you have now, so the process can go on. The clouds are still spreading. It is not yet time to act.

Transforming Lines

Initial nine: Return to the source. Go your own way. How could that be a mistake? This generates meaning and good fortune by releasing transformative energy. *Direction:* Gently penetrate to the core of the problem. Turn potential conflict into creative tension. The situation is already changing.

Nine at-second: Something important returns and you are pulled back to it like an animal on a rope. This generates meaning and good fortune by releasing transformative energy. Stay in the centre. Don't let go of this source. *Direction:* Find a supportive group. Stay inside it. This is a place where others can join you. Gather energy for a decisive new move.

Nine at-third: The cart is stopped by the spokes in the wheels. Stirring people up and trying to carry a big load has brought on a family quarrel. Husband and wife are exasperated, rolling their eyes at each other and looking in opposite directions. You can't put your home in order like this. *Direction:* Find your own centre before you try to move on. Take things in. Provide what is needed. Be open to new ideas.

Six at-fourth: Have confidence. You are connected to the spirits and they will carry you through. If you act, you can leave the possibility of bloodshed and loss behind. You are not making a mistake. Your purpose will unite you with those above you. *Direction:* Take action. You are connected to a creative force.

Nine at-fifth: Have confidence. You are connected to the spirits and they will carry you through. Acting now will connect you with others. Take hold of things. Your neighbours are a source of riches you can use. Don't try to accumulate things alone. *Direction:* Be active. Find an idea that brings people together. Turn potential conflict into creative tension. The situation is already changing.

Nine above: The rain has come. Stay where you are for now. You have honour, capacity and the power to realize things. If you act as a wife, confined to household duties, you will face difficulties. There is an angry spirit there, seeking revenge for past mistreatment. Use the image of the moon that is almost full. Don't go past the midpoint in anything you do. Don't discipline or punish people, no matter how good your motives. The power behind the situation is still amassing the capacity to carry you forward. If you try to take control and reduce things to order, you will be cut off from the spirits and left open to danger. There is still something dubious and uncertain here. *Direction:* Wait for the right moment to move. Turn potential conflict into creative tension. The situation is already changing.

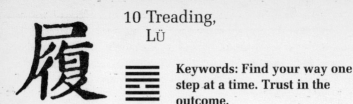

10 Treading, LÜ

Keywords: Find your way one step at a time. Trust in the outcome.

Treading describes your situation in terms of how you find and make your way. The way to deal with it is to proceed step by step. The path is there. Practise. Think about the right way to act and how to gain your livelihood. You are walking in the tracks of a tiger, a powerful and dangerous being. If you are careful, this being will give you what you need to exist and frighten off what is trying to harm you. Speak with it and partake of its power and intelligence. Don't do anything to make it bite you and don't snap at people yourself. You can't afford to sneer and scold. This is pleasing to the spirits. Through it they will give you success, effective power and the capacity to bring the situation to maturity.

> **Tread,** LÜ: Walk, step; path, track, way; shoes; walk on, walk in the tracks of, follow a path; act, practise, accomplish; conduct, behaviour; salary, means of subsistence; happiness, luck; the paths of the stars and planets. The ideogram portrays a person's feet walking.

The hexagram figure shows an outer struggle met by cheerful self-expression. Heaven is above, the mists are below. Find supportive people. Everyone must amass enough to live on. You must find the right way to do this. Don't stay where you are. Treading and finding your way is the foundation of your ability to realize the *tao*. It harmonizes and develops your capacity to move in accord with the way. Carefully differentiate what is above you and what is below you. Set your purpose right. Clarify your relation to the desires that everyone holds in common. The inner stimulation to movement that you feel now can connect you with a powerful creative force. It is like treading on a tiger's tail. If you don't want the tiger to bite you, refrain from snapping at people yourself. The centre of your desire is solid and correct. You are walking with the highest power. Don't be disheartened. Continuing your efforts to illuminate the situation will bring a real change in awareness.

Transforming Lines

Initial nine: Go your way simply. Be pure in your intent. This is not a mistake. You are moving with your desire. *Direction:* Argue your position but don't act on it. Find a supportive group. Stay inside it. Gather energy for a decisive new move.

Nine at-second: You are treading the *tao.* Smooth and even things through continual efforts. If you are hidden away or working on a secret project, put your ideas to the trial. This generates meaning and good fortune by releasing transformative energy. Accept concealment. Your desire is properly centred. It does not originate in confusion or a desire to cause trouble. *Direction:* Stay unentangled. Re-imagine your problems. Gather energy for a decisive new move.

Six at-third: It is true that if you squint through one eye, you can still see. If you limp, you can still walk on. But your capacities are so diminished in this situation that you can't see or act clearly. In such case, treading on the tiger's tail will cut you off from the spirits and leave you open to danger. The tiger will bite you. You will find yourself surrounded by nasty, critical people. You are like a simple soldier who is trying to act for a great commander. Your position doesn't give you clarity or the capacity to move freely. Act with resolve and purpose only if you have received strict orders from someone you truly respect. *Direction:* You are confronting a powerful and dangerous force.

Nine at-fourth: You tread on the tiger's tail. It listens to you and helps you. State your case fully and with fervour. Bringing your idea to completion generates meaning and good fortune by releasing transformative energy. Your purpose is truly moving. *Direction:* Connect your inner and outer life. Take things in. Be open to new ideas. Provide what is needed.

Nine at-fifth: Go on your way resolutely, even if you must leave something behind. You are confronting difficulties. An angry old ghost has returned to seek revenge for past mistreatment. Take action. Correcting your situation is the right thing to do. *Direction:* Turn potential conflict into creative tension. The situation is already changing.

Nine above: Look at the path you have been treading. There are omens there. Your predecessors are extending their blessings. Consult them. This path recurs again and again. Following it is the source of great good fortune and meaningful events. Here you reach the source of things at the top. Your purpose and ideas bring great rewards. *Direction:* Join with others and express yourself. Find a supportive group. Stay inside it. Gather energy for a decisive new move.

11 Pervading, T'AI

Keywords: Expand, communicate, connect, enjoy.

Pervading describes your situation in terms of an influx of spirit that brings flowering and prosperity. The way to deal with it is to spread the prosperity and good feeling by communicating it. You are connected to the flow of energy. Be great, abounding and fertile. What is unimportant is departing, along with the necessity to be small and adapt to whatever crosses your path. The time that is coming offers you the chance to develop your fundamental ideas. It generates meaning and good fortune by releasing transformative energy. This is pleasing to the spirits. Through it they will give you success, effective power and the capacity to bring the situation to maturity.

Pervade, T'AI: Great, eminent, abundant, prosperous; peaceful, fertile; reach everywhere, permeate, diffuse, communicate; smooth, slippery; extreme, extravagant, prodigious. Mount T'ai was where great sacrifices were made that connected heaven and earth. The ideogram portrays a person in water, connected to the flow of the *tao*.

The hexagram figure shows a creative force pervading the earth. Heaven and earth come together. This is a time of abundance. Let yourself be led to realize your hidden potential. Later you can be quiet and settled. Reach out and penetrate things. Sense their interconnections. Radically change your sense of yourself and who you associate with. Put your possessions at the service of the spirit of the time. Support and encourage people. Use peace and abundance to set life in order. This is a time when the fundamental powers mingle with humans and all the beings connect with one another. What is above and what is below come together. Your purpose is in accord with them. Be firm and focused inside and adaptable in your dealings with the world. Stay connected with the *tao* through using the oracle. You are surrounded by people who are continually adapting to whatever brings them advantage. Their way is now dissolving. Your way will endure.

Transforming Lines

Initial nine: Whatever is bothering you, pull it up by the roots. It is twisted together and confused. It is keeping you from advancing. Change who you associate with and how you think about yourself. Putting things in order and setting out on an expedition generates meaning and good fortune by releasing transformative energy. Locate your purpose outside yourself. Let it take you into the world. *Direction:* Make the effort. Turn potential conflict into creative tension. The situation is already changing.

Nine at-second: You are surrounded by a wasteland. Ahead of you lies a river. Cross it on your own. Don't hesitate to abandon current relations that are holding you back. You will acquire honour this way, for the centre of things is moving. *Direction:* Accept the coming hardship. In the end your light will shine through. Release bound energy. The situation is already changing.

Nine at-third: After level, peaceful times come difficult times. Things fall apart and you must climb the rising slope. But if you don't let go of what you are holding on to, it will never be able to return. You are facing a difficult task in a time when others seem to be enjoying better things. This is not a mistake. Don't worry. Act this way with confidence. You are connected to the spirits and they will carry you through. Take in what is coming. It brings you blessings and goodwill. *Direction:* An important connection is coming nearer. It is the return of something significant. Don't take the lead. Be open to new ideas. Provide what is needed.

Six at-fourth: You are fluttering around like a little bird trying to leave the nest. If you don't have the resources to accomplish what you want to do, call on your neighbours, family or friends. Don't be defensive. Act on your idea with confidence. You are connected to the spirits and they will carry you through. Let go of your desire for immediate gain. Centre and stabilize what your heart desires. *Direction:* This idea is full of invigorating strength. Be resolute. You arc connected to a creative force.

Six at-fifth: The great ancestor gives a maiden in marriage. This is an omen of future happiness. It begins the burgeoning time of early spring. It can gratify desires, fulfil needs and realize your aims. It is the source of great good fortune and meaningful events. You can use this new connection to act on your ideas and desires, but it will take time. *Direction:* Wait for the right moment to act. Turn potential conflict into creative tension. The situation is already changing.

Six above: The walls collapse into the moat. The prosperous city falls. Don't organize your forces to combat it. Notify your own people. This has fate behind it. Putting your ideas to the trial would only bring shame and humiliation. Your destiny is in disarray. *Direction:* Find a new idea to concentrate your energy. Turn potential conflict into creative tension. The situation is already changing.

12 Obstruction, PI

Keywords: Stop! Beware, communication is blocked.

Obstruction describes your situation in terms of being blocked or interfered with. The way to deal with it is to stop what you are doing and accept the obstruction. Communication is cut off. You are connected with the wrong people. If you try to act, you will encounter misfortune. Your proposals will be rejected. You will be personally disapproved of. There is no way for someone who wants to stay in touch with the *tao* to take advantage of this situation. What is important is departing, along with your ability to realize your plans. The time that is coming is small and mean. You will have to adapt to it. Don't seek to impose your ideas. Retreat and be patient.

> **Obstruct,** PI: Closed, stopped, bar the way; obstacle; unable to advance or succeed; deny, refuse, disapprove; bad, evil, unfortunate, wicked, unhappy. The ideogram portrays a mouth and the sign for not. It suggests blocked communication.

The hexagram figure shows a struggle in the outer world that blocks expression. Heaven and earth do not come together. Proceed step by step. You can't always be part of a group. Change your sense of yourself and who you normally associate with. Don't mingle. Be careful about what you become involved with. Avoid heavy work or responsibility. If you avoid honours and don't display yourself, you can continue to draw benefits from the situation. What is happening is not your fault. Deal with it impersonally. It is a time of disconnection and isolation in which you do not have a real field of activity. Be humble and flexible inside yourself, but erect firm barriers outside. What is worthy is being excluded from centres of power, which are run by people who seek their own advantage. Their way will endure for now. The way of those who uses the oracle to stay in touch with the *tao* is dissolving.

Use this advice and diminish your involvements. They can bring you no advantage now.

Transforming Lines

Initial six: Whatever is bothering you, pull it up by the roots. It is twisted together and confused and is keeping you tied up in the situation. Change who you associate with and how you think about yourself. Putting your ideas to the trial generates meaning and good fortune by releasing transformative energy. Follow what you believe in. *Direction:* Stay unentangled. Proceed step by step. Gather energy for a decisive new move.

Six at-second: Wrap up what you receive. Keep it secret and nourish it like a child in the womb. Adapt to whatever crosses your path. Be polite to those around you. This generates meaning and good fortune by releasing transformative energy. Your ideas and your ability to realize them are obstructed, but they are growing. Make an offering to the spirits. They can give you success, effective power and the ability to bring the situation to maturity. Don't make the people around you nervous. *Direction:* Argue your position but don't act on it. Find a supportive group. Stay inside it. Gather energy for a decisive new move.

Six at-third: Taking on responsibility will only embarrass you. This may come from an awareness of an inner fault, or simply because the situation is not appropriate. In any case, don't do it. *Direction:* Pull back, retreat. This will couple you with a creative force.

Nine at-fourth: You have a mandate from fate. Continue on through obstruction and isolation. You will experience great happiness and spread light and awareness. There is no mistake here. Your purpose is moving. *Direction:* Contemplate the whole field of action. Strip away old ideas. Be open to new ones. Provide what is needed.

Nine at-fifth: Let the obstructions go. Take a break. This generates meaning and good fortune by releasing transformative energy. Focus on your central idea. The bad time is ending. It won't return. Imagine yourself in a peaceful and luxuriant rural retreat. This is the appropriate place for you. It will correct the whole situation. Relax and enjoy yourself. *Direction:* You will slowly and surely emerge into the light. Re-imagine the situation. Gather energy for a decisive new move.

Nine above: The obstruction is turned on its head. What was at first a block is now a cause for rejoicing. The time of obstruction is over. Let it flow away. Why go on regretting things? *Direction:* Gather people and resources for a great new project. Proceed step by step. Gather energy for a decisive new move.

13 Concording People, T'ung Jen

Keywords: Assemble, co-operate, unite for a common goal.

Concording People describes your situation in terms of sharing something with others. The way to deal with it is to find ways to unite the people involved. This is the kind of task that can best be done together and brings mutual advantage in the end. Find places of agreement where goals can be shared. Develop group spirit and a bond of common understanding. This is pleasing to the spirits. Through it they will give you success, effective power and the ability to bring the situation to maturity. This is the right time to embark on a significant enterprise or enter the stream of life with a goal. Use the oracle and put your ideas to the trial.

> **Concord,** T'UNG: Harmonize, bring together, unite; union, concord, harmony; equalize, assemble, share, agree; together, held in common; the same time and place. The ideogram portrays a mouth and the sign for cover. It suggests silent understanding and things that fit together.

People, JEN: Human beings; an individual; humanity. The ideogram portrays a person kneeling in prayer or submission.

The hexagram figure shows warmth and understanding that help people in their struggles. Heaven united with fire. You are connected to a creative force. People should not remain isolated from one another. Think about the ways to connect them. Sort people out by giving them rallying points and finding common ancestors. You can succeed in this situation by being flexible and adaptable. This leads you to the centre and puts you in contact with the creative force moving there. Say it like this: Bring people together, for creative force is moving in the situation. Persist in your efforts to illuminate the inherent beauty of things. Put central emphasis on not going to one extreme or the other. Use the oracle to stay in touch with the *tao*. This enables you to connect with the deep purposes that influence and move the human world.

Transforming Lines

Initial nine: People are gathering at the gate. You are about to cross over the threshold. This is not a mistake. Take action. Walk through the door. Where is the fault in that? *Direction:* Leave this situation. It will couple you with a creative force.

Six at-second: People are gathering in front of their ancestors, in the presence of what they look up to. You feel the shame and confusion of having lost the way. This is precisely the right feeling to have. Let it induce reflection and correct how you are thinking about the situation. *Direction:* Take action. You are connected to a creative force.

Nine at-third: Hide your weapons in the thick undergrowth. Climb the hill to the tombs of your ancestors, the place where you can think about things and find help. You are facing a very strong antagonist. You will not be able to act for quite a while. *Direction:* Stay unentangled. Proceed step by step. Gather energy for a decisive new move.

Nine at-fourth: Ride on your ramparts, the protection you have built up. No one can succeed in attacking you. Take vigorous action. Rouse things up by stimulating vital power and desire. This generates meaning and good fortune by releasing transformative energy. It will reverse what looks like a confining situation. *Direction:* Stay inside your group. Gather energy for a decisive new move.

Nine at-fifth: People who gather together may cry and wail at first, but soon they will laugh and rejoice. Having a cause turns them into an organized unit that can take effective action. Proceed directly. Speak plainly and sincerely. Correct the extremes. Using words can bring this group together and empower them. *Direction:* Spread awareness and warmth. Don't be afraid to act alone. You are connected to a creative force.

Nine above: People are gathering at the edges of the city. There is no cause for sorrow. This group doesn't have a purpose yet. *Direction:* If you want things to go anywhere, you will have to peel off the dead skin. Take action. You are coupled with a creative force.

14 Great Possessing,
TA YU

Keywords: A time to be great. Concentrate, produce and share the results.

Great Possessing describes your situation in terms of acquiring great abundance and prosperity through the development of a central idea. The way to deal with it is to concentrate your energies in one place and share the fruits of your efforts. Focus on a single idea and impose a direction on things. Be noble and magnanimous with the results. This can be a continuing source of fertility and excellence. It is pleasing to the spirits. Through it they will give you success, effective power and the capacity to bring the situation to maturity. Make a great offering and share with others.

> **Great,** TA: Big, noble, important; able to protect others; orient your will towards a self-imposed goal; the ability to lead or guide your life; yang energy.

> **Possess,** YU: There is; to be, to exist; have, own; possessions, goods; dispose of; arise, occur, events. The ideogram portrays a hand holding an offering. It suggests sharing with the spirits and other people.

The hexagram shows a concentrated inner force that spreads brightness and warmth. Fire above heaven. This is a time of creative abundance. Be resolute. You can associate with people and convert them to your ideas. You can gather crowds around you. Firmly check hatred in order to bring out what is virtuous and usable. Yield and work with the spirit above and let go of your personal limits. What is flexible and adaptable has acquired the ability to give honour to things. This will bring your idea to the centre of attention. What is above and what is below respond to it. This is what is called great possessing. You can realize the *tao* through firm persistence. Make the inherent beauty of things brighter and brighter. This connects you with heaven above and with the right time to do things. It is pleasing to the spirits. Through it they will give you success, effective power and the capacity to bring the situation to maturity.

Transforming Lines

Initial nine: There is no harm to yourself or others involved in this undertaking. You are definitely not making a mistake. The very hard work involved is also not a mistake. This is the beginning of a great endeavour. *Direction:* You can re-imagine the world and build something enduring. Be resolute. You are connected to a creative force.

Nine at-second: Use a great vehicle to carry great ideas. Develop the ability to carry out your plans. Impose your ideas.

Have a direction. This is not a mistake. Amass strength in the centre. This will not harm things, nor will it end in defeat. *Direction:* Spread awareness and warmth. Don't be afraid to act alone. You are connected to a creative force.

Nine at-third: Concentrate what you are working on. Collect what you have grown. Present it to the highest principle you know of, like a noble making a gift to the Son of Heaven. This creates a firm connection. Don't be flexible and adaptable. Don't let other people control your ideas. That would be harmful now. *Direction:* Turn potential conflict into creative tension. The situation is already changing.

Nine at-fourth: This is not a time to be forceful or domineering. You will not succeed in enforcing your ideas on others. Be very clear about this. Share things. Let others shine. This is not a mistake. *Direction:* Gather energy for a great undertaking. If you let yourself be led, you can realize a hidden potential. The situation is already changing.

Six at-fifth: The spirits are certainly with you! As soon as you meet people, you impress them with the strength and sincerity of your ideas. Act with confidence. The spirits will carry you through. This generates meaning and good fortune by releasing transformative energy. Stay true to your ideas and expand your purpose. Your power to impress has real meaning and will further your good fortune. Be versatile and stay imaginatively open instead of trying to prepare things. *Direction:* You are directly in contact with a creative force.

Nine above: This idea originates in heaven, the spirit power above, which will shield and protect both it and you. There is nothing for which it will not, ultimately, be advantageous. It generates meaning and good fortune by releasing transformative energy. Your idea possesses the greatest significance. It is protected and blessed by the power of the spirit. *Direction:* Invigorate yourself. Be resolute. You are connected to a creative force.

15 Humbling / Holding Back, CH'IEN

Keywords: Think and speak humbly to accomplish your goals.

Humbling/Holding Back describes your situation in terms of cutting through pride and complication. The way to deal with it is to keep your words and thoughts simple and connected to fundamental things. Think and speak of yourself in a modest way. Take the lower position. By yielding you acquire the power to realize the *tao*. This is pleasing to the spirits. Through it they will give you success, effective power and the capacity to bring the situation to maturity. If you use the oracle to keep in touch with the *tao*, you can complete what you want to do. Your acts will not bring things to an end, but will open new possibilities. Cutting through pride and the need to dominate brings a great power of realization. Be clear about this, then act directly.

> **Humble,** CH'IEN: Think and speak of yourself in a modest way; voluntarily give way to others, polite, modest, simple, respectful; yielding, compliant, reverent. The ideogram portrays spoken words and the sign for unite. It suggests keeping words connected to the facts.

The hexagram figure shows an inner limit that connects you to the power of the earth. In the middle of the earth there is a mountain. This will release you from constraint and bring creative balance. Don't go to extremes. Be agile and alert. Humbling gives you a handle on the power to realize who you are meant to be. It dignifies and clarifies things, cutting away formality by keeping rules simple and clear. Reduce the many to augment the few. Carefully appraise the value of things to equalize the flow of energy. This is a time of connection between the spirit powers. Heaven moves below to bring brightness and clarity. Earth's modesty moves in the above. Heaven's way is to lessen what is overfull and augment what is humble. Earth's way is to transform what is overfull and spread what is humble. The souls and spirits who govern the world harm what is overfull and bless what is humble. The people's way is to hate what is overfull and love what is humble. Humbling brings dignity and makes things shine. It is modest and does not try to go beyond what is there. Through it you can accomplish and complete things.

Transforming Lines

Initial six: Hold back. Be very humble. Think everything through twice. Use the oracle to help you stay in touch with the *tao*. Use this attitude to embark on your new enterprise. Step into the stream of life with a purpose. This generates meaning and good fortune by releasing transformative energy. Stay below the common level. *Direction:* Accept the difficult time. It will deliver you from your problems. The situation is already changing.

Six at-second: Let your power speak through modest words. It will call out to others, like the song of birds through which they recognize their kind. Putting your ideas to the trial generates meaning and good fortune by releasing transformative energy. Make a statement from the centre of your heart and you can obtain what you wish for. *Direction:* Make the effort. If you let yourself be led, you can realize a hidden potential. The situation is already changing.

Nine at-third: Humbly carry on with the work. Exert yourself without advertising your efforts. Use the oracle to stay in touch with the *tao*. Bringing your plan to completion generates meaning and good fortune by releasing transformative energy. It mobilizes an undeveloped potential outside your normal set of values that will attract many people. *Direction:* Don't take the lead. Provide what is needed.

Six at-fourth: There is nothing for which this will not, ultimately, be advantageous. It inaugurates a very fertile period. Show your ideas and achievements humbly and without attachment. It is important not to get involved in arguments.

Don't impose your will. *Direction:* Proceed carefully at first. Don't be afraid to act alone. You are connected to a creative force.

Six at-fifth: No false modesty here. Take action. If you don't have the resources to do what you want to do, use your neighbour's, your family's or your friends'. Invade and subjugate things by whatever means necessary, openly or by stealth. That brings profit and insight. There is nothing for which this will not, ultimately, be advantageous. Discipline, punish, put things in order. This is not a time to submit. *Direction:* Re-imagine the situation. Gather energy for a decisive new move.

Six above: Let your power speak through modest words. It will call out to others, like the song of birds through which they recognize their kind. Mobilize your forces and attack the cities and provinces. You haven't yet acquired what you set out for. The time is right to get it. Mobilize your forces and attack. *Direction:* Go on until you reach a natural boundary. Release bound energy. The situation is already changing.

16 Providing for / Responding, Yü

**Keywords: Prepare now.
You will enjoy it later.**

Providing for/Responding describes your situation in terms of gathering what is needed to meet and enjoy the future. You can deal with it by accumulating strength and resources so you can respond spontaneously and fully when the time comes. Prepare things. Take precautions. Think things through so you can move smoothly with the flow of events. It is like riding an elephant that you have previously tamed, a creature of great grace and power. Establish and empower helpers, so your forces can be easily mobilized to respond to any situation. That brings profit and insight.

Provide for/Respond, Yü: Ready, prepared for; take pre-cautions, arrange, make ready; happy, content, rejoice, take pleasure in; carried away, enthusiastic, respond immediately, ready to explode. The ideogram portrays a child riding an elephant. It suggests that being prepared lets you respond spontaneously.

The hexagram figure shows accumulated energy bounding forth at a sudden call to action. Thunder comes from earth impetuously. Re-imagine the situation. Humbly amass a great store of things to provide for what comes. Then you don't have to worry. Double the gates and establish the watch so you are ready for violent visitors. That way you understand what the situation means. When thunder came bursting forth from the earth, the rulers of earlier times were ready. They aroused delight, made music and thus honoured the power to realize the *tao.* They exalted the highest spirit and thus became very wise. Have a firm purpose and act on it. Yield and build up the capacity to spontaneously respond to a stimulus. This is why the old world worked so well. This is why you should estab-lish helpers to mobilize your forces. This is the way heaven and earth work together, how they create time and order the seasons. The old wise people acted like this. They could respond immediately from their store of power to punish what was clearly wrong and thus the people accepted them. The time of providing for responding is both righteous and great.

Transforming Lines

Initial six: Don't call out to others in order to build up what you need. You will be cut off from the spirits and left open to danger. Your purpose will be exhausted. Wait and respond to a real stimulus. *Direction:* A fertile shock is coming. Re-imagine the situation. Gather energy for a decisive new move.

Six at-second: The limits you have set for yourself are turning you to stone. Don't even complete one more day. Putting your ideas to the trial generates meaning and good fortune by releasing transformative energy. Make correcting your position your central concern. *Direction:* Release bound energy. The situation is already changing.

Six at-third: Don't be sceptical and don't procrastinate. Whatever you have to provide for, do it or you will most certainly be sorry. This situation is not appropriate. *Direction:* Be very careful at the beginning. Don't be afraid to act alone. You are connected to a creative force.

Nine at-fourth: The reserves are there to meet the challenge. Have no doubts. You will acquire what you desire and the power to express what is important to you. You will join people together like cowries strung on a thread or a hair clasp gathering the hair. Your purpose can move great things. *Direction:* Don't take the lead. Be open to new ideas. Provide what is needed.

Six at-fifth: You are confronting affliction, sickness, disorder, anger or hatred. Keep on. It won't kill you. You are riding a firm, persisting force. Your centre has not been extinguished. *Direction:* Gather things and people for a great new endeavour. Proceed step by step. Gather energy for a decisive new move.

Six above: You are groping in the dark and you are misinformed about the situation, which will probably change for the worse. The only thing you can accomplish here is to deny false assertions and connections. The situation isn't your fault, but it is obscuring your values. Why let it go on any longer? Climb out of the cave. *Direction:* You will slowly and surely emerge into the light. Re-imagine the situation. Gather energy for a decisive new move.

17 Following, SUI

**Keywords: Don't fight it.
Go with the flow**.

Following describes your situation in terms of been drawn forward. The way to deal with it is to follow the inevitable course of events. Go with the flow. Yield to the path set out in front of you. Be guided by the way things are moving. You are involved in a series of events that are firmly connected. Don't fight it, move with it. It opens a whole new cycle of time. This is not a mistake. The situation cannot harm you. This is pleasing to the spirits. Through it they will give you success, effective power and the capacity to bring the situation to maturity.

> **Follow,** SUI: Come or go after in an inevitable sequence; conform to, according to, come immediately after; in the style of, according to the ideas of; move in the same direction; follow a way, school or religion. The ideogram portrays three footsteps, one following the other.

The hexagram figure shows an outer stimulus rousing inner energy. In the middle of the mists there is thunder. Proceed step by step. When you have provided for the call, it comes. Let go of what is past, all the old quarrels and sorrows that led up to this situation. Dim your discriminating power so old mental habits can dissolve. A firm new focus is emerging, called up by an outer stimulus. This great new idea is pleasing to the spirits. Through it they will give you success, effective power and the ability to bring the situation to maturity. This is not a mistake. Put it to the trial. The whole human world must follow the times and the seasons. What you are actually following is a righteous idea inherent in the time.

Transforming Lines

Initial nine: Deny the office or position you now occupy and go out through the gate. Leave your old beliefs behind. Putting your ideas to the trial generates meaning and good fortune by releasing transformative energy. Mingling with others gets real work done. *Direction:* Gather things and people for a great new project. Re-imagine the situation. Gather energy for a decisive new move.

Six at-second: You have attached yourself to the small child and let go of the responsible manager. You are alone, without associates, and must adapt to whatever crosses your path. *Direction:* Be cheerful and express yourself. Find a supportive group. Stay inside it. Gather energy for a decisive new move.

Six at-third: You are have attached yourself to the responsible manager and have let the small child go. Following this way, you can seek out and acquire what you desire. Continue in what you are doing. It will bring profit and insight. Take a firm grip on your purpose. *Direction:* Change the way you present yourself. It will couple you with a creative force.

Nine at-fourth: You are following something in order to catch it. This is not the right way to do it. It will cut you off from the spirit and leave you open to danger. Think about this, and change your approach. Follow the *tao* and brighten your awareness. Have confidence. This links you to the spirits and they will carry you through. How could that be a mistake? Your righteous sense of purpose is leading you astray. Don't be so eager to control things. The proper thing to do is to locate yourself in the *tao* and have confidence that it will bring you what you need. Then you will understand what achievement really means. *Direction:* This is an important new beginning. Strip away your old ideas. Be open to the new. Don't take the lead. Provide what is needed.

Nine at-fifth: You are linked to the spirits and they will carry you through. You are moving towards excellence. Have confidence in this. Act sincerely and truly. This will generate meaning and good fortune by releasing transformative energy. The situation is correctly centred. *Direction:* Stir things up and act. Gather energy for a decisive new move.

Six above: You are firmly attached to what you are following. Through you the other followers are held together. You are enshrined in the hall of memories and become one of the ancestral spirits. This is as far as you can go. *Direction:* Stay unentangled. Re-imagine the situation. Gather energy for a decisive new move.

18 Corruption / Renovating, KU

Keywords: Beware! Search out the source of corruption.

Corruption/Renovating describes your situation in terms of poison, putrefaction, black magic, and the evil deeds done by parents that are manifested in their children. The way to deal with it is to help things rot away so that a new beginning can be found. You are facing something that has turned to poison. Search out the source so new growth can begin. This is pleasing to the spirits. Through it they will give you success, effective power and the capacity to bring the situation to maturity. This is the right time to enter the stream of life with a goal, or to embark on a significant enterprise. That brings profit and insight. Prepare the moment when the new time arrives and carefully watch over its first growth. It will take three days, a whole period of activity, before the seed of the new energy bursts open, and a similar period afterwards to stabilize it.

Corrupt/Renovating, KU: Rotting, poisonous; intestinal worms, venomous insects; evil magic; seduce, pervert, flatter, put under a spell; disorder, error; business. The ideogram portrays poisonous insects in a jar used for magic.

The hexagram figure shows an obstacle in the outer world that turns inner growth back on itself. Below the mountain there is wind. If you let yourself be led, you can realize a hidden potential. Doing business always implies corruption. If you find its source, you can stabilize the situation. Rouse up the undeveloped potential outside your normal set of values in order to nurture the power to realize what you must do. A solid limit above is stopping the nourishment of new growth. This means corruption. This rotting away can be the beginning of a new spring. Make the effort. This is pleasing to the spirits. Through it they will give you success, effective power and the capacity to bring the situation to maturity. You can regulate the world anew. Set out with a firm purpose. You will soon have enough to keep you busy. There will be three days before the seed of the new bursts open, and three days afterwards. Watch carefully. You can bring things to a conclusion that results in a new beginning. The spirit above is moving in this situation.

Transforming Lines

Initial six: You are dealing with a father's corruption, which has to do with exercising authority. Accept being a son. Consult with the old wise men. This is not a mistake. You are facing a difficult time. There is an angry ghost here that has returned to take revenge on the living. Going through this difficulty generates meaning and good fortune by releasing transformative energy. Be intent on examining what has gone before you. Look at how gifts and commands were received and how orders were carried out. If you avoid getting caught up in the corruption, your predecessors will remain without fault. Make this your central concern. *Direction:* Concentrate, focus, be active. If you let yourself be led, you can realize a hidden potential. The situation is already changing.

Nine at-second: You are dealing with a mother's corruption, which has to do with nourishing children. Divination can't help you. Putting your ideas to the trial won't help either. Find the centre of the situation and put yourself in the *tao.*

Direction: Finding and articulating the obstacle releases bound energy. The situation is already changing.

Nine at-third: You are dealing with a father's corruption, which has to do with exercising authority. You will regret it if you simply adapt to the situation. It would be a mistake not to have your own ideas. Bringing things to completion is not a mistake. *Direction:* There is something you are not aware of in the situation. Don't take the lead. Provide what is needed. Be open to new ideas.

Six at-fourth: You are adding to a situation corrupted by the father, which has to do with the exercise of authority. If you go on in this way, you will see yourself covered with shame and humiliation. You haven't got what you need yet. *Direction:* Transform your awareness of the situation. Be resolute. It will connect you with a creative force.

Six at-fifth: You are dealing with a father's corruption, which has to do with exercising authority. Use praise, eulogies, even flattery to deal with the situation. You can earn praise in this way yourself, and receive the power to realize your inherent destiny. *Direction:* Gently penetrate to the core of the problem. Turn potential conflict into creative tension. The situation is already changing.

Nine above: It is not your job to be the vassal of a king. Don't get involved in business or politics. Your job is to find and prize what is excellent. Thus you acquire your real purpose. This is the place of those who work on in the darkness to provide for a coming awakening. *Direction:* Make the effort. If you let yourself be led, you can realize your hidden potential. The situation is already changing.

19 Nearing, LIN

Keywords: The point of new arrival. Welcome what is approaching.

Nearing describes your situation in terms of something approaching, particularly something great approaching something smaller. It is the first arrival and point of new contact. The way to deal with it is to move towards what is approaching without expecting to get what you want immediately. Look at things with care and sympathy. Welcome the approach of others. Keep your expectations modest. This contact opens a whole new cycle of time. It is particularly favourable for what is growing. So beware. Trying to rush to completion and an early harvest will cut you off from the spirits and leave you open to danger.

> **Nearing,** LIN: Approach, behold with care and sympathy; commanded to come nearer; look down on sympathetically, confer favour and blessing; inspect; arrive, the point of arrival, make contact; honour or be honoured by a visit.

The hexagram figure shows desire for contact expressed through a willingness to work and serve. Above the mists there is earth. This is the return of the great. Invite it to come nearer. The proper thing to do is to bring things together. When you teach, use your teaching to continually ponder the heart's concerns. Tolerate and protect things and people outside your normal set of values without setting limits on them. There is an undeveloped potential there that you rely on without knowing it. What is strong and firm in this situation increases gradually. Work to express it. Keep yourself centred and connected to things. If you want something great to come of this, you must continually correct yourself. That is heaven's way. Stay on an even path. Trying to rush to completion and an early harvest will cut you off from the spirits and leave you open to danger. The whole situation will dissolve.

Transforming Lines

Initial nine: A stimulating and inspiring connection is coming nearer. It puts things together that belong together. Putting your ideas to the trial generates meaning and good fortune by releasing transformative energy. Your purpose is moving and correcting itself. *Direction:* Organize your forces. This is the return of something important. Be open to the new. Provide what is needed.

Nine at-second: A stimulating and inspiring connection is coming nearer. It will connect things that belong together. This generates meaning and good fortune by releasing transformative energy. There is nothing for which this will not, ultimately, be advantageous. You haven't realized all the ramifications of this yet. *Direction:* This is the return of something important. Be open to it. Don't take the lead. Provide what is needed.

Six at-third: Something sweet is coming nearer. However agreeable it may seem, there is no way good can come of it. The situation is simply not appropriate. If you have already realized this and are grieving over it, don't worry. No lasting harm will result. *Direction:* This change in your thinking will begin a flourishing new time. Turn potential conflict into creative tension. The situation is already changing.

Six at-fourth: The climax is coming nearer. This is not a mistake. The time is right. Go for it. *Direction:* Turn potential conflict into creative tension. The situation is already changing.

Six at-fifth: Knowledge is coming nearer. This belongs to a great chief, one who can influence and help people through the power of a great idea. It generates meaning and good fortune by releasing transformative energy. This can change the central way you see yourself and what is important to you. *Direction:* Assimilate and articulate this. Find your voice. Take things in. Provide what is needed.

Six above: Wealth, honesty and generosity are coming nearer. You can come nearer to what you desire through these qualities. This generates meaning and good fortune by releasing transformative energy. It is not a mistake. Hold on to your inner purpose. *Direction:* Decrease your present involvements to make new energy available. Actively curb your anger. Something important is returning. Provide what is needed. Be open to new ideas.

20 Viewing,
KUAN

Keywords: Let everything come into view. Divine the meaning.

Viewing describes your situation in terms of the need to look without acting in order to find the right perspective. The way to deal with it is to let everything emerge and divine the central meaning. Particularly, look at what you usually don't want to see or think about. This figure describes a particular moment in a religious ceremony, when the purification has been made and the libation is about to be poured out. Have confidence. Examining things will bring you the insight you need. When you have made the preparations, the spirit will arrive and carry you through.

> **View,** KUAN: Contemplate, look at from a distance or height; examine, judge, conjecture about; divination; idea, point of view; instruct, inform, point out, make known; *also:* A Taoist monastery, an observatory, a tower. The ideogram portrays a bird and the sign for see. It suggests a bird's-eye view and watching bird signs.

The hexagram figure shows images appearing on the inner field. The wind moves above the earth. Strip away your old ideas. There is something of great importance here, and you can seek it out. The early rulers used this time to inspect the borders. They contemplated the needs of the people and set up ways to instruct them. Take a high view of the matter at hand. Yield to things and give them space on the inner ground. Stay correctly centred and you can let the whole world come into view. If you prepare things well, the spirit will answer and carry you through. The things you are trying to influence will change spontaneously. By viewing the way that heaven moves through the spirits, you can see the proper times for things. When the sages used the way of the spirits to establish and teach, the whole human world would listen.

Transforming Lines

Initial six: You are viewing things like a young person. This is not a mistake if you are flexible and have nothing you want to do. If you want to use the oracle to stay in touch with the *tao*, it means you have lost the right way. *Direction:* Increase your efforts. Strip away old ideas and be open to new ones. Provide what is needed.

Six at-second: You are observing from hiding, peeping through the screen. This is the traditional woman's place, secretly viewing and influencing things. If you accept this, it can bring profit and insight even though you may see shameful things. *Direction:* Clear away obstacles to understanding. Take things in. Don't take the lead. Provide what is needed.

Six at-third: View your life and what you give birth to. Watch the flow as it advances and retreats. Set your question in this context and see where it comes from. Then decide whether or not to act. Don't let go of the *tao*. *Direction:* Proceed step by step. Gather your energy for a decisive new move.

Six at-fourth: You are viewing the shining of a great city. You have been invited to an important advisory position without having real power. Take advantage of invitations from those above you and honour your guests. That brings profit and insight. *Direction:* Communication is obstructed. Beware of being pulled into compromising situations. Proceed step by step. Gather energy for a decisive new move.

Nine at-fifth: View your life and what you give birth to. Set your question in this context and see where it comes from. Use the oracle to help you. Then decide whether or not to act. This is not a mistake. *Direction:* Strip away old ideas and be open to new ones. Don't take the lead. Provide what is needed.

Nine above: View the lives and the origins of those around you. Imagine yourself as one of them. Set your question in this context and see where it comes from. Use the oracle to help you. Then decide whether or not to act. This is not a mistake. Your purpose is not yet in order. *Direction:* Change who you associate with and how you categorize things. Strip away old ideas and be open to new ones. Provide what is needed.

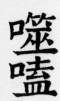

21 Gnawing and Biting Through, SHIH HO

Keywords: Confront the problem. Bite through the obstacle.

Gnawing and Biting Through describes your situation in terms of confronting a tenacious obstacle. The way to deal with it is to gnaw away what is unnecessary and bite through the core of the problem. Something is keeping the jaws from coming together. Take decisive action. Gnaw away at the obstacles until you reach the hidden centre, then bite through what is keeping things apart. This is pleasing to the spirits. Through it they will give you success, effective power and the capacity to bring things to maturity. Take things to court. That brings profit and insight. This is a time for legal action, punishment and a warning against criminal activity.

Gnaw, SHIH: Bite away, chew, eat; nibble, bite persistently; arrive at, attain; reach the truth by removing what is unessential. The ideogram portrays a mouth and the sign for divination. It suggests finding the truth by divining what is hidden.

Bite, HO: Unite, bring together; close the jaws, bite through, crush, chew; the sound of voices. The ideogram portrays a mouth and a covered vessel. It suggests the jaws coming together as a lid fits a pot.

The hexagram figure shows inner determination breaking through obstacles and spreading clarity. Thunder and lightning. Gather your forces. Re-imagine the situation. You have contemplated long enough. Take resolute action. You have the opportunity to bring things together. Provide what is needed. This is a severe time. The early kings used it to clarify criminal punishments and thus enforce the laws. There is something between the jaws. Say it this way: Gnaw and bite through! This is pleasing to the spirits. Through it they will give you success, effective power and the capacity to bring the situation to maturity. Decide when to be adaptable and when to be firm. Stir things up and clarify them. Create a structure that unites thunder, the shock that comes from below, and lightning, the sudden clarity that comes from above. Keep your centre flexible and act from above. Even though the situation may not be appropriate, bringing things to judgement brings profit and insight.

Transforming Lines

Initial nine: You are wearing stocks for shoes. Your feet disappear. This keeps you from moving for now. This is not a mistake. *Direction:* You will slowly and surely emerge into the light. Re-imagine the situation. Gather your energy for a decisive new move.

Six at-second: You are very enthusiastic. Gnawing through flesh, your nose disappears. This is not a mistake. Don't be afraid to lose face. Keep on. You are riding a strong solid force. *Direction:* Turn potential conflict into creative tension. The situation is already changing.

Six at-third: Gnawing though dried meat, you encounter something poisonous. This is old, tough, nasty stuff. Don't simply let it go by. You will lose the right way. This is not a mistake. *Direction:* Clarify the situation. Don't be afraid to act alone. You are connected to a creative force.

Nine at-fourth: Gnawing through meat that has been parched on the bone. Examine the results of past efforts. You acquire the ability to give things form and to direct your strength. This is the beginning of a creative endeavour. Accept drudgery and difficulty. That brings profit and insight. Putting your ideas to the trial generates meaning and good fortune by releasing transformative energy. Things aren't clear yet, so keep on working. *Direction:* Take in what has happened before. Provide what is needed.

Six at-fifth: Gnawing through parched meat. This is a long, arduous task. You will acquire wealth and the possibility to establish a line of descent. You are facing an angry old ghost who returns to take revenge for past mistreatment. Go through the difficult time. This is not a mistake. You will acquire what you need. *Direction:* Don't get entangled in other people's problems. Proceed step by step. Gather energy for a decisive new move.

Nine above: Why are you putting your head in the stocks? Your ears disappear and you can't hear anything. This cuts you off from the spirits and leaves you open to danger. Think again. You most certainly won't be enlightened this way. *Direction:* You may be in for quite a shock. Re-imagine the situation. Gather energy for a decisive new move.

22 Adorning,
Pı

Keywords: Beautify things and be brave.

Adorning describes your situation in terms of its outward appearance. You can deal with it by decorating, beautifying and embellishing the way things are presented. This builds up intrinsic value. Be elegant. Be brilliant. Display your valour. Let the way you present yourself signal the changes in your life. This is pleasing to the spirits. Through it they will give you success, effective power and the capacity to bring the situation to maturity. Be flexible and adapt to what presents itself to be done. Have a place to go. Impose a direction on things. That brings profit and insight.

> **Adorn,** PI: Embellish, ornament, beautify; elegant, brilliant, ornamented; inner worth seen in outer appearance; energetic, brave, eager, passionate, intrepid; display of courage. The ideogram portrays cowrie shells, a sign of value, and flowers. It links worth and beauty.

The hexagram figure shows an outer limit that produces a radiant display. Beneath the mountain there is fire. Release tensions and display energy. People can't come together carelessly. They must be embellished to be seen. At present you lack a means of expression. Brighten and clarify all the different parts of how you present yourself. Don't cut off social and legal processes that are already underway. Adorning things is pleasing to the spirits. Through it they will give you success, effective power and the capacity to bring the situation to maturity. Be adaptable. This reveals the strength of the underlying design and its source. Then having a plan or imposing a direction brings profit and insight. It reveals heaven's design. Brightening and clarifying the pattern, and stopping there, reveals it to the people involved. Contemplate the overall pattern. Look at the transformation the seasons can bring. Contemplate the pattern of the people involved. Use gradual, continuous change to accomplish things in the human world.

Transforming Lines

Initial nine: Adorn your feet. Be brave. Put what you ride on aside. Walk on your own two feet. This is definitely the right thing to do. *Direction:* Stabilize your situation by finding the limits. This releases bound energy and delivers you from distress. The situation is already changing.

Six at-second: Adorn your beard. Be brave and be patient. The connection with a superior is already there. It will lift you into significant new activity. *Direction:* Collect your forces. Prepare for a very active time. If you let yourself be led, you can realize hidden potential. The situation is already changing.

Nine at-third: Adorn yourself with this idea. Soak it up. Let it impregnate you. By putting this idea to the trial you generate a continual source of meaning and good fortune. If you don't try to bring it to an end, it will provide for those who come after you. *Direction:* Take things in. Be open to new ideas. Don't take the lead. Provide what is needed.

Six at-fourth: Respect this idea. Adorn it with old and venerable grey hair. There is a white horse inside it that can give you the strength to fly high and manifest creative energy. Whatever is approaching is not out to harm you. It is more like an offer of marriage. Though you may have real cause to doubt, don't use force. Make alliances. Bring things to completion without going overboard. *Direction:* Spread light and warmth. Don't be afraid to act alone. You are connected to a creative force.

Six at-fifth: You are on your way to adorn the tombs and monuments. As you climb the hill to the graves, you realize you have very little to present. The roll of silk with your writing on it is small, very small. You become aware that you have lost the right way. Don't despair. Let this induce reflection and correct the way you are living your life. Going through with your plan generates meaning and good fortune by releasing transformative energy. It gives you a cause to rejoice. *Direction:* Find a supportive group. Stay inside it. Gather energy for a decisive new move.

Nine above: Adorn yourself in white, the colour of death and mourning, autumn and harvest, the colour of what is clear, plain and pure. This is not a mistake. Acquire a noble purpose. *Direction:* Accept the difficult time. It will release bound energy and deliver you from sorrow. The situation is already changing.

23 Stripping, PO

Keywords: Strip away old ideas and habits.

Stripping describes your situation in terms of habits and ideas that that are outmoded and worn out. The way to deal with it is to strip away what has become unusable. This brings renewal. Remove and uncover things. Cut into the problem and strip away the unessential without thought of immediate gain. If you can do that, then you can impose a direction on things or have a place to go.

Strip, PO: Flay, peel, skin, scrape, slice; remove, uncover, take off; reduce, diminish; reduce to the essentials; prune trees, slaughter animals. The ideogram portrays a knife and the sign for carving. It suggests taking decisive action to cut something away.

The hexagram figure shows the end of a cycle and the preparation for the new. The mountain rests on the earth. Be open to new ideas. Provide what is needed. Re-establish creative balance by stripping away outmoded embellishments. There is something rotten here. Take action. Give generously to what is below to stabilize your position. Stripping away the old implies someone to carry it out. You need a base. What is flexible and adaptable is transforming what is solid and firm, so it is not advantageous to impose a direction on things. Those who adapt to what is coming will endure. Yield to the situation and stop what you have been doing. Concentrate on the symbolic value of things, their power to connect you with the world of the spirits. Use the oracle to stay in touch with the *tao*. This is a time when old structure dissolves so new action can emerge. Fill the empty, fertile inner space to overflowing. Heaven is moving there.

Transforming Lines

Initial six: Wake up! Strip the bed, your resting place. Change your stand on things and your views about what supports you. If you ignore this and continue on as you are, you will be cut off from the spirits and be left open to danger. *Direction:* Take the situation in. Provide what is needed. Be open to new ideas.

Six at-second: Wake up! Strip the bed, your resting place, by clearly dividing yourself from others. Mark off your space. Dispute things. Bite into the matter at hand. If you ignore this and continue on as you are, you will be cut off from the spirits and left open to danger. You don't have the proper associates yet. *Direction:* Don't act out of ignorance. Something significant is returning. Be open to new ideas.

Six at-third: Strip it away! This is not a mistake. Let everything go. *Direction:* You have reached the limit. This time is over. Release bound energy. The situation is already changing.

Six at-fourth: If you try to strip the bed, your resting place, you will cut into your own flesh. You will wound yourself and others. Don't do it. It will cut you off from the spirits and leave you open to danger. You are slicing close to a calamity here. *Direction:* You will slowly and surely emerge into the light. Re-imagine the situation. Gather energy for a decisive new move.

Six at-fifth: String the fish together. Profit and fertility are hidden in the stream of changing events that stripping has revealed. You can catch what you want and need. Those who live within the house will confer their grace and favour on you. Honour them. Use your connections and trust your imagination. There is nothing for which this will not, ultimately, be advantageous. *Direction:* Let everything emerge into view. Strip away your old ideas and be open to new ones. Don't take the lead. Provide what is needed.

Nine above: There is a ripe fruit that hasn't been eaten. Take in the results of your actions. Use the oracle to stay in touch with the *tao*, and carry it away with you. If you simply adapt to the situation, your shelter will be stripped away. Stay in touch with what is outside your normal set of values. There is a capacity there that will carry you through. You cannot accomplish anything by simply staying where you are. *Direction:* Be open to new ideas. Don't take the lead. Provide what is needed.

24 Returning, Fu

Keywords: Go back and welcome the new beginning.

Returning describes your situation in terms of re-emergence and re-birth. The way to deal with it is to go back to meet the returning energy in order to begin anew. Retrace your path, return to the source, re-establish what is important, restore the way. Find the intensity of the earlier time and the purity of the original feeling. This is pleasing to the spirits. Through it they will give you success, effective power and the capacity to bring the situation to maturity. Let things emerge and come back without pressure or upset. People will suggest mutually profitable projects. It is not a mistake to join them. Turning and moving in the opposite direction from your former path will return you to the way on the seventh day. Have a place to go. Impose a direction on things. That brings profit and insight.

> **Return,** Fu: Go back, turn back, return to the starting point; come back, reappear; resurgence, re-birth, renaissance; re-establish, renew, renovate, restore; again, anew; an earlier time and place; the very beginning of the new time. The ideogram portrays walking and the sign for retracing a path.

The hexagram figure shows inner energy returning to the field of activity. Thunder in the earth. Be open to new ideas and provide what is needed. The old situation has been stripped away. Turn in your tracks and go back to meet what is re-emerging. This return to the way is the root of your power to realize *tao* in action. Be small, adaptable and differentiate yourself from others. Use your own knowledge of the source of things. To nurture this returning energy, early rulers would close the frontiers and the markets at the time of the solstice. Merchants and sojourners would not move. The prince would not go on tours of inspection. This kind of attention is pleasing to the spirits. Through it they will give you success, effective power and the capacity to bring the situation to maturity. What is strong and firm is reversing itself. Stir things up and work with the movement. Let things emerge and come back without pressure or upset. People will suggest mutually profitable projects. It is not a mistake to join them. Turning and moving in the opposite direction from your former path will return you to the way. On the seventh day, the return will come. Heaven is moving here. Impose a direction, have a place to go, for the strong and firm will endure. By returning, you see the heart of the union of heaven and earth.

Transforming Lines

Initial nine: Don't put off returning. Don't simply repent past confusion. The way is very close. Take the step. This is the source of great good fortune and meaningful events. It renovates your whole being. *Direction:* Be open to new ideas. Don't take the lead. Provide what is needed.

Six at-second: Returning through relinquishing. Let go of what you are doing and return to the way. This generates meaning and good fortune by releasing transformative energy. Be unselfish and benevolent. Recognize your common humanity. *Direction:* An important connection is approaching. Be open to new ideas. Don't take the lead. Provide what is needed.

Six at-third: Something is pressing, urgent to return. This is a critical moment. You are confronting an angry old ghost that returns to take revenge for past mistreatment. Going through this difficult time is not a mistake. It is the right thing to do. *Direction:* Accept the difficult time. It will release bound energy and deliver you from your problem. The situation is already changing.

Six at-fourth: Move to the centre. Return to yourself. Accept being alone. You follow the *tao* by doing this. *Direction:* Prepare for a fertile shock. Re-imagine the situation. Gather energy for a decisive new move.

Six at-fifth: Act on your plans. Generosity, honesty and wealth will return to strengthen you. You will have no cause to regret. The old wise men are behind you. *Direction:* Give everything a place to grow. Strip away old ideas and be open to new ones. Provide what is needed.

Six above: Delusion, infatuation, confusion and deception return to bewitch and blind you. If you act on your idea you will be cut off from the spirits and left open to danger. It brings disaster from within and without. If you try to move your forces this way, they will be completely ruined. Their leader will be cut off and destroyed. It will take ten years to bring the repercussions of this disaster under control. It will completely reverse your ability to influence things. Take this advice in. Think about where your desire came from. *Direction:* Take the situation in. Don't take the lead. Be open to new ideas.

 ## 25 Without Embroiling, WU WANG

 Keywords: Disentangle yourself, then trust your intuition.

Without Embroiling describes your situation in terms of acquiring the capacity to act spontaneously and confidently. The way to deal with it is to free yourself from disorder. Disentangle yourself from compulsive ideas, confusion, vanity, anger, lust, hatred and the desire for revenge. By freeing your awareness from these entanglements, you gain the capacity to act directly. This opens up a whole new cycle of time. If you do not correct yourself, you will consistently make mistakes through ignorance and faulty perception. Your sight will be clouded. Imposing a direction on things or having a place to go will bring you no advantage.

Without, WU: Devoid of, not having.

Embroiling, WANG: Caught up in, entangled, emeshed, involved; vain, rash, reckless, foolish, wild; lie, deceive; idle, futile, without foundation, false; brutal, insane, disordered.

The hexagram figure shows new actions inspired by the spirit above. Below heaven, thunder is moving. Proceed step by step. The spirit has really returned. If you return to it, you will not be the source of disaster. Associate with others without getting caught up in disorder. The early rulers, whose virtue was strong, used this flourishing time to nourish the myriad beings. Firmness and strength have come from the outside to activate a central principle within you. Respond and persist in this connection. This solid purpose is central and links you with the spirits. By staying in touch with it and continually correcting yourself, you can begin a great period of growth, effective power and enjoyment. Heaven will bestow it as fate. If you do not correct yourself, you will consistently make mistakes through your own ignorance and faulty perception. Imposing a direction or having a place to go will bring you no advantage. If you lose the capacity to act in accord with the spirits, how can you do anything right? Heaven will not protect you. Disentangle yourself. Do it now!

Transforming Lines

Initial nine: Act, but don't get entangled. Simply let the present situation go. This generates meaning and good fortune by releasing transformative energy. You acquire a new purpose. *Direction:* Communication is blocked. You are connected to the wrong people. Proceed step by step. Gather energy for a decisive new move.

Six at-second: Don't cultivate this crop, don't clear this land. This is not the right time or place to make long-term efforts. If you realize this, imposing a direction or having a place to go will be advantageous. You aren't wealthy yet. *Direction:* Go your own way step by step. Find a supportive group. Stay inside it. Gather energy for a decisive new move.

Six at-third: This unfortunate occurrence isn't your fault. You can stay unentangled if you see it in the right way. Perhaps there was an ox tied to a post. Perhaps someone who lived in the city was very attached to this ox. If someone on the move was to acquire this ox, the city dweller would think it was a disaster. The traveller, however, would acquire new strength and capacity. Take your pick. Stay or move. *Direction:* Unite for a common goal. There are new connections to be made. They will couple you with a creative force.

Nine at-fourth: This is an enabling divination. Whatever you are thinking of, put it to the trial. This is not a mistake. It does no one harm. You are firmly in possession of the situation. *Direction:* Increase your efforts and involvements. Pour on the coal. Strip away old ideas. Provide what is needed.

Nine at-fifth: The sickness, disorder, anger or hatred you are facing now is not your fault. If you do not attack it on the literal level, you will ultimately have cause to rejoice. Don't experiment with these kinds of remedies at all. *Direction:* Search out the real obstacle and bite through it. Re-imagine the situation. Gather energy for a decisive new move.

Nine above: Stay unentangled. To act on your plan would be a mistake. You are ignorant of the real situation. Do not impose a direction or have a place to go. If you do act like this, you will only exhaust yourself and bring on a disaster. *Direction:* Follow the obvious flow of events. Proceed step by step. Gather energy for a decisive new move.

26 Great Accumulating, TA CH'U

Keywords: Concentrate, focus, be active.

Great Accumulating describes your situation in terms of having a central idea that defines what is valuable. The way to deal with it is to focus on a single idea and use that to impose a direction on your life. Concentrate everything on this goal. Gather all the different parts of yourself and all your many encounters. Take the long view. Think of yourself as raising animals, growing crops or bringing up children. Tolerate and nourish things. Develop an atmosphere in which things can grow. Putting your ideas to the trial brings profit and insight. It can culminate in great abundance. Don't stay at home. Be active. Take in what is coming. This generates meaning and good fortune by releasing transformative energy. This is the right time to enter the stream of life with a purpose or to embark on a significant enterprise.

Great, TA: Big, noble, important; able to protect others; orient your will towards a self-imposed goal; the ability to lead or guide your life; yang energy.

Accumulate, CH'U: Gather, collect, take in, hoard, retain; control, restrain; take care of, support, tolerate; tame, train or pasture animals; raise, bring up, domesticate; be tamed or controlled by something. The ideogram portrays fertile black soil accumulated by retaining silt.

The hexagram figure shows creative force accumulating within. Heaven in the centre of the mountain. If you let yourself be led, you can realize your hidden potential. Put your purpose in order and use it as an accumulating point. It is the right time to act. Assimilate the records of what your many predecessors have done and go on from there. Accumulate the power to realize things. Be firm, persist. Your efforts to shed light on things will bring you glory and substantial rewards. Renew your power, your virtue and your connection to the *tao* every day. Have a firm overriding purpose. Honour what has moral and intellectual power. Stabilize what endures and correct your focus. Don't stay at home. Taking in what comes generates meaning and good fortune by releasing transformative energy. It nourishes intellectual and moral power. This is the right time to step into the stream of life with a purpose. The connections reach to heaven.

Transforming Lines

Initial nine: This situation is possessed by an angry old ghost that returns to take revenge for past mistreatment. Bring your involvement to an end. Decline the challenge and get out of the way of coming disaster. That brings profit and insight. *Direction:* This situation is corrupt. If you let yourself be led out of it, you can realize a hidden potential. The situation is already changing.

Nine at-second: The cart is stopped by the axle-straps, the connection between the body and the wheels. Relationships have broken down, and you can't carry on. Stay in the centre. Don't go to extremes and don't try to compete. *Direction:* Adorn and embellish things. This will release bound energy and deliver you from the problem. The situation is already changing.

Nine at-third: Mounted on a fine horse, in pursuit of your goals. If you can accept drudgery and difficulty, put your ideas to the trial. This is difficult work when you feel others are better off than you are. Imagine it like this: you are escorting a precious hidden cargo. Impose a direction. Have a place to go. That brings profit and insight. Unite your purpose with a higher goal. *Direction:* See present hardship as the source of future gain. Diminish involvements and decrease emotions. This is the return of something important. Be open to it. Provide what is needed.

Six at-fourth: Collect young cattle in a stable. Attach a form to their heads to protect the growth of their horns. Accumulate the strength to carry heavy loads and the force to confront difficult situations. This is the source of great good fortune and meaningful events. It will give you cause to rejoice. *Direction:* This begins a time of creative power and abundance. Be resolute. You are connected to a creative force.

Six at-fifth: The tusks of a gelded boar. What could be a fierce enemy has been deprived of the power to do harm. This generates meaning and good fortune by releasing transformative energy. It will bring you rewards. *Direction:* Accumulate small things to achieve something great. Turn potential conflict into creative tension. The situation is already changing.

Nine above: Isn't this the road of the heavenly spirits? Your idea pleases them. Through it they will give you success, effective power and the capacity to bring things to maturity. Isn't this the way heaven moves? The way is moving in your idea. *Direction:* This begins a flourishing and productive time. If you let yourself be led, you can realize your hidden potential. The situation is already changing.

27 The Jaws / Swallowing, Yı

Keywords: Take in what has happened. Provide nourishment.

Jaws/Swallowing describes your situation in terms of what goes in and out of an open mouth. The way to deal with it is to take things in to provide for yourself and others. Take in what has been said and done and let it nourish the new. Provide what is necessary to feed yourself and those connected with you. Putting your ideas to the trial generates meaning and good fortune by releasing transformative energy. Contemplate what nourishes people and what you are nourishing. Think about what you give and what you ask for. Seek out the source of what goes in and out of your mouth and the mouths of others. The answer to your question lies there.

Jaws/Swallowing, YI: Mouth, jaws, cheeks, chin; eat, take in, ingest; feed, nourish, sustain, bring up, support; provide what is necessary; what goes in or out of the mouth. The ideogram portrays an open mouth.

The hexagram figure shows previous accomplishments being swallowed to nourish new growth. Within the mountain, there is thunder. Provide what is needed. After beings are brought together, they must be nourished. Correct the way things are nourished, and nourish the ability to correct things. Consider your words carefully when you speak with others. Articulate how you eat, drink and take things in. Putting your ideas to the trial generates meaning and good fortune by releasing transformative energy if you use them to correct how things are nourished. Contemplate the open mouth. Look at where and how things are nourished. Look at the source of your own nourishment. Heaven and earth nourish the myriad beings. The sages nourish what is excellent in order to extend it to others. This is truly a time to be great.

Transforming Lines

Initial nine: You set the soul-tortoise aside and sadly contemplate your crestfallen face. You have let go of the whole world of the imagination, your magic, your protection, your ability to see what is coming. No wonder you look so sad and undernourished. Taking this stance has no value whatsoever and can give you no support. It cuts you off from the spirits and leaves you open to danger. *Direction:* Strip away your old ideas and be open to new ones. Don't take the lead. Provide what is needed.

Six at-second: Your connection to what can nourish you is disturbed and toppling over. You are rejecting the rules and standards, departing from the norms. Head for the place you can take this in and think about it, the site of your own graves and shrines. Trying to discipline others or setting out on an expedition would cut you off from the spirits and leave you open to danger. *Direction:* Diminish your involvements and curb your anger. This can lead to new awareness. Something important is returning. Be open to it. Provide what is needed. Don't take the lead.

Six at-third: You are rejecting what nourishes you. This cuts you off from the spirits and leaves you open to danger. If you go on like this, you won't be able to act again for ten years. There is no way this can be advantageous. Your central idea goes directly against the *tao. Direction:* Put a brave face on it and let go of your plans. Release bound energy. Deliver yourself. The situation is already changing.

Six at-fourth: Your connection to the source of nourishment is disturbed and toppling over. Find a new one. This generates meaning and good fortune by releasing transformative energy. Be like a tiger, full of force and concentration. When you look, look hard and eagerly. When you desire something, pursue it and don't stop pursuing. This zeal is not a mistake. You spread light over everything through your efforts. *Direction:* Bite through the obstacles that confront you. Re-imagine the situation. Gather energy for a decisive new move.

Six at-fifth: You are rejecting the rules and standards, departing from the norms. Stay where you are and put your ideas to the trial. This generates meaning and good fortune by releasing transformative energy. This is not the right time to enter the stream of life with a goal or to embark on a significant enterprise. You are yielding to an impulse that connects you to what is above. *Direction:* A fertile new time is coming. Strip away your old ideas and be open to new ones. Provide what is needed.

Nine above: You are nourished by what has come before you. Look into what has happened in the past. You are confronting a difficult situation. An angry old ghost has returned to take revenge for past mistreatment. Going through these difficulties generates meaning and good fortune by releasing transformative energy. This is the right time to enter the stream of events with a purpose, or to embark on a significant enterprise. Your central idea will be rewarded. *Direction:* Something significant is returning. Be open to it. Provide what is needed.

28 Great Exceeding, TA KUO

Keywords: A crisis. Gather all your force. Don't be afraid to act alone.

Great Exceeding describes your situation in terms of how to act in a time of crisis. The way to deal with it is to push your principles beyond ordinary limits and accept the movement it brings. Have a noble purpose. Find what is truly important and organize yourself accordingly. The ridgepole of your house is warped and sagging. The structure of your life is in danger of collapse. But there is a creative force at work in this breakdown. So impose a direction on things. Have a place to go. This is pleasing to the spirits. Through it they will give you success, effective power and the capacity to bring things to maturity.

> **Great,** TA: Big, noble, important; able to protect others; orient your will towards a self-imposed goal; the ability to lead or guide your life; yang energy.

> **Exceed,** KU: Go beyond; pass by, pass over, surpass; overtake, overshoot; get clear of, get over; cross the threshold, surmount difficulties; transgress the norms, outside the limits; too much.

The hexagram figure shows outer contacts overwhelming inner penetration. The mists submerge the ground. There is a creative force at work in this breakdown. If your situation doesn't nourish you, if it can't stir up new growth, push it over and leave. Don't be afraid to order things by yourself. Don't be sad about retiring from the community. Having a great idea means being excessive. The structure of your life is warped and sagging. The roots and the tips, the places where you make contact and are nourished, are fading. Let the strong force gathering in the centre penetrate and stimulate movement. Impose a direction on things. Have a place to go. This is pleasing to the spirits. Through it they will give you success, effective power and the capacity to bring things to maturity. This is a very great time.

Transforming Lines

Initial six: Prepare your move carefully. Spread an offering mat beneath it. Be clear, pure and concentrate on essentials. Remember that great things have humble beginnings. You are below in this situation. Be flexible and adaptable. *Direction:* Be resolute. You are connected to a creative force.

Nine at-second: A withered willow gives birth to new shoots. An old husband acquires a young consort. Something is added to a worn out situation that results in a burst of new growth. This new connection brings help in a time of crisis. *Direction:* This influence connects what belongs together. It couples you with a creative force.

Nine at-third: The structure you are living in fails. The ridge-pole buckles, the house collapses. This will cut you off from the spirits and leave you open to danger. There is no way to brace the situation up. *Direction:* If you go on like this, you will be totally isolated. Find a supportive group. Stay inside it. Gather energy for a decisive new move.

Nine at-fourth: The ridgepole is crowned. The structure you live in is braced and strengthened. Its virtues are unfolded and displayed. This generates meaning and good fortune by releasing transformative energy. When the situation has been stabilized, don't try to go any further. Trying to add to it only brings humiliation and regrets. The tension has been dispersed and the connection made. *Direction:* Find your relation to the things that everyone needs. If you let yourself be led, you can realize a hidden potential. The situation is already changing.

Nine at-fifth: A withered willow gives birth to flowers. An old wife acquires a young husband. Something is added to a worn out situation that results in a brief burst of beauty. There is neither praise nor blame involved. Enjoy it. It won't last long.

Direction: Continue on your way. Be resolute. You are connected to a creative force.

Six above: If you go beyond wading in these waters, you will go under. You will be cut off and left open to danger, through no fault of your own. You must choose how far you want to involve yourself. It is not a question of fault or blame. It reflects something bigger than everyday concerns. Decide what sort of action you want to take. *Direction:* Be resolute. You are connected to a creative force.

29 Repeating Gorge/Venturing, Hsi K'an

Keywords: Collect your forces. Take the risk. Do it again and again.

Repeating Gorge/Venturing describes your situation in terms of repeatedly confronting something dangerous and difficult. The way to deal with it is to take the risk without holding back. You cannot avoid this obstacle. Conquer your fear and faint-heartedness. Jump in, like water that pours into a hole, fills it up and flows on. Practise, train, accustom yourself to danger. This is a critical point. It is a pit that could trap you and become a grave. But there is no way around it. Summon your energy and concentration. Repeatedly confront the challenge. You can act this way with confidence, for you are linked to the spirits and they will carry you forward. Hold fast to your heart and its growth. This is pleasing to the spirits. Through it they will give you success, effective power and the capacity to bring the situation to maturity. Moving, acting, motivating things will bring you honour, so give them first place.

> **Repeat,** Hsi: Practise, rehearse, train, coach; again and again; familiar with, skilled; repeat a lesson; drive, impulse. The ideogram portrays wings and a cap. It suggests thought carried forward by repeated movements.

> **Gorge,** K'AN: A dangerous place; hole, cavity, pit, hollow; steep precipice; snare, trap, grave; a critical time, a test; take risks; *also:* Venture and fall, take a risk without reserve at the key point of danger. The ideogram portrays a deep hole in the earth into which water flows.

The hexagram figure shows water repeatedly flowing into the gorge. Streams continually reach the goal. Take in the situation. Overflowing energy from your central idea is moving toward the depths. Act on your principles. When you teach and when you act, repeat things again and again. Redouble your efforts, spread your energies. Don't get caught in one place. Gather your desires and hold on to your heart's growth. Then you will have a solid centre. Moving and acting will bring honour. Push on and achieve things. Gorge means danger. Heaven's dangers cannot be ascended. Earth's dangers are its mountains and rivers, its hills and mounds. Kings and their vassals set up dangers to guard their cities. A danger confronted and used is both an accomplishment and a defence. Now is the time to concentrate your forces and take risks.

Transforming Lines

Initial six: Repeating the gorge, you are caught in the pit. By responding to the same challenge again and again, you get caught in a dead end, a fatal diversion. It cuts you off from the spirits and leaves you open to danger. The *tao* is slipping through your fingers. *Direction:* Set limits to your efforts. Find a voice. Take the situation in. Provide what is needed.

Nine at-second: You encounter a difficult passage. Take the risk. Seek out what you need. You will acquire it by being flexible and adaptable. Don't let go of the centre yet. *Direction:* Change who you are associating with. Strip away your old ideas and be open to new ones. Provide what is needed.

Six at-third: Gorge after gorge, challenge after challenge is coming at you. Take it easy at first. If you enter the gorge now, you will get trapped in a dead end, a fatal diversion. Don't do it. You won't achieve anything. Are you sure you know what you want? *Direction:* Look for the source of your values. If you let yourself be led, you can realize your hidden potential. The situation is already changing.

Six at-fourth: If you are trapped in the gorge, don't fight it. Lay out a meal for the spirits. Offer a cup with liquor, the distillation of your efforts. Set out two clay vessels, the symbols of your body. Open yourself to the imagination and the answer will come in through the window. It will illuminate your dark situation and give you the instructions you need. You are at the border, where events emerge. *Direction:* This will move you out of isolation. Find a supportive group. Stay inside it. Gather energy for a decisive new move.

Nine at-fifth: Not too much, don't fill it to overflowing; the water in the gorge is already rising. This is not a mistake. Stay in the centre. Don't make a great effort. *Direction:* Organize your forces. Something important is returning. Be open to it. Provide what is needed.

Six above: Bound with stranded ropes and sent off to the dense thorn bushes to be judged and found wanting. This idea is wrong. If you go on like this, you won't get anywhere for three years. You will be cut off from the spirits and left open to danger. Why are you letting go of the *tao? Direction:* Dispel illusions. Take the situation in. Don't try to lead. Be open to new ideas. Provide what is needed.

30 Radiance / Clarifying, LI

Keywords: Articulate and spread the light and warmth.

Radiance/Clarifying describes your situation in terms of awareness and coherence. The way to deal with it is to articulate and spread light and warmth. Illuminate, articulate, discriminate, make things conscious. Bring together what belongs together.

This is a time of intelligent effort and accumulating awareness. It includes unexpected and meaningful encounters, separations from the old and experiences outside the ordinary. Put your ideas to the trial. That brings profit and insight. It is pleasing to the spirits. Through it they will give you effective power, enjoyment, and the capacity to bring things to maturity. Accumulating the receptive strength that can carry burdens generates meaning and good fortune by releasing transformative energy.

> **Radiance,** LI: Spreading light; illuminate, discriminate, articulate, arrange and order; consciousness, awareness; leave, separate yourself from, step outside the norms; two together, encounter by chance; belong to, adhere to, depend on; *also:* Brightness, fire and warmth. The ideogram portrays a magical bird with brilliant plumage.

The hexagram figure shows awareness enduring and spreading. Brightness doubled arouses Radiance. Concentrate your energy. You have fallen and found bottom. Now the time calls for bringing things together. Radiance shines above you. Connect your idea with this brightness and use it again and again to spread clarity and care to the four corners of the world. Radiance means connecting and illuminating. The sun and moon connect with and illuminate heaven. The many grains, grasses and trees connect with and illuminate the earth. Brightening things again and again reinforces correcting. This is how change occurs in the world. Being flexible and adaptable connects you with what is central and correct. It is the source of growth and is pleasing to the spirits. That is why accumulating the receptive strength that can carry burdens generates meaning and good fortune by releasing transformative energy.

Transforming Lines

Initial nine: Polish and clarify the beginning. Proceed step by step. Keep a hold on yourself. Respect things. Inquire into motives. Get rid of your own faults first. Then you won't make a mistake. *Direction:* Search outside the norms. Don't be afraid to act alone. This can connect you to a creative force.

Six at-second: Yellow radiance glows in this idea, light and power from the centre in the earth. This is the source of great good fortune and meaningful events. You acquire the centre and connect with the way. *Direction:* A great idea and a creative time are coming. Be resolute. You are connected to a creative force.

Nine at-third: You are seeing things in the light of the sun going down. Instead of beating your drums or singing your songs, you sit there like a very old person lamenting all the terrible things that have happened in your life. This cuts you off from the spirits and leaves you open to danger. Why go on like this? *Direction:* Bite through the obstacles. Proceed step by step. Gather your energy for a decisive new move.

Nine at-fourth: This comes on like a brush fire or a sudden assault. It burns up, dies and you can throw it away. Forget it. A flash in the pan. It doesn't have a place in your life. *Direction:* Put on a happy face. Re-imagine the situation. Gather energy for a decisive new move.

Six at-fifth: Cry over this as if your sorrow would never end. Mourn over this as if the memory will haunt you forever. This generates meaning and good fortune by releasing transformative energy. You have lost your central relationship. But the connection is still there underneath it all. *Direction:* Find a supportive group. Stay inside it. You are coupled to a creative force.

Nine above: The king sends out troops to punish the rebels. This is an excellent thing to do. Sever the head and let the demons go. Take what is imaginatively important and let go of painful memories and feelings. The opposition will fall apart and you will be freed from shame. This generates meaning and good fortune by releasing transformative energy. It corrects the order of things. *Direction:* This ushers in a time of abundance. Don't be afraid to act alone. You are coupled to a creative force.

31 Conjoining,
HSIEN

Keywords: Be open to the influence. Bring things together.

Conjoining describes your situation in terms of an influence that excites, mobilizes or triggers you into action. The way to deal with it is to find the best way to bring things together. This influence is working to unite the separated parts of something that belongs together. Reach out, join things, allow yourself to be moved. This is pleasing to the spirits. Through it they will give you success, effective power, enjoyment, and the capacity to bring the situation to maturity. Put your ideas to the trial. That brings profit and insight. The woman and the yin are the keys to the situation. Understanding, accepting and acting through the woman generates meaning and good fortune by releasing transformative energies.

> **Conjoin,** HSIEN: Contact, influence, move; excite, mobilize, trigger; all, totally, universal, continual, entire; unite, bring together the parts of a previously separated whole; come into conjunction, as the planets; *literally:* A broken piece of pottery, the two halves of which were joined to identify partners.

The hexagram figure shows inner strength submitting to outer stimulation. Above the mountain there are the mists. Accept what is coming as the sign of something greater. This reflects the way the world is made. When heaven and earth conjoin, the myriad beings appear; when man and woman conjoin to become husband and wife, the generations appear; when chief and servant conjoin, what is above and what is below are properly ordered. Relations are clarified and individuals have a way to order their hearts. Bring things and people together through emptiness, the empty yet fertile space within you. Make peace, spread satisfaction and agreement. Something is indeed influencing and exciting you. Through it you can move the hearts of others. The flexible and adaptable is above, the firm and persistent is below. They excite and invoke each other, moving through mutual interaction. The man is below, the woman above. Accepting, understanding and submitting to the woman and the yin is pleasing to the spirits. Through it they will give you success, effective power, profit and insight. When heaven and earth influence each other this way, the myriad beings change and give birth. When the sage influences people's hearts this way, the world is harmonized and made even. Contemplate the place where things can be influenced and touched. By doing so you can see what moves the hearts of heaven, earth and the myriad beings.

Transforming Lines

Initial six: The impulse stimulates your big toes. This is what starts you walking. The influence comes from far and is in its beginning. Locate your purpose outside yourself. *Direction:* This will bring revolution and renewal. Change the way you present yourself. You are coupled with a creative force.

Six at-second: The impulse stimulates your calves. Though you want to change your stance, stay where you are. This generates meaning and good fortune by releasing transformative energy. If you start running, you will fall into a pit. You will be cut off from the spirits and left open to danger. Yield and stay free of harm. *Direction:* Don't be afraid to act alone. You are connected to a creative force.

Nine at-third: The impulse stimulates your thighs. Don't let it run away with you. Hold on to your desire to follow it. If you follow this influence, you lose the way. This will not last. Stay where you are and find your purpose in the people who follow you. This is a time to hold on to what is below. *Direction:* Gather people together for a great new project. Proceed step by step. Gather energy for a decisive new move.

Nine at-fourth: Take action on this impulse. Putting your ideas to the trial generates meaning and good fortune by releasing transformative energy. All cause for regret will be extinguished. The impulse wavers back and forth, so you may be indecisive. Simply think about it deeply and the help you need will arrive. You are not yet connected to anything harmful, and your central idea is not entirely clear. *Direction:* Re-imagine the situation. Gather energy for a decisive new move.

Nine at-fifth: The impulse stimulates the muscles along your spine, neck and shoulders. This is a deep connection. It will bring no cause for regrets. You are feeling the tips of something that will manifest over time. *Direction:* Be very careful at the beginning. Don't be afraid to act alone. You are connected to a creative force.

Six above: The impulse stimulates your jaws, cheeks and tongue; your mouth produces a torrent of words that have a stimulating effect. This won't last long. *Direction:* Retire, pull back. It will couple you with a creative force.

32 Persevering, HENG

Keywords: Continue on. Renew your efforts.

Persevering describes your situation in terms of what continues and endures. The way to deal with it is to continue on the way you are going. Be constant, regular, stable. Persist in your normal way of life and what you feel is right. This is pleasing to the spirits. Through it they will give you success, effective power and the capacity to bring things to maturity. Proceeding in this way is not a mistake. Put your ideas to the trial. Impose a direction on things. Have a place to go. These things bring profit and insight.

Persevere, HENG: Continue in the same way or spirit; constant, stable, regular; enduring, perpetual, durable, permanent; self-renewing; ordinary, habitual; extend everywhere, universal; the moon when it is almost full.

The ideogram portrays a heart and a boat between two shores. It suggests enduring in the voyage of life.

The hexagram figure shows arousing energy coupled with inner penetration. Thunder and wind. This is a time for resolute action. It is the way of the husband and wife. It implies that things endure over time. Persevering fixes and steadies the power to realize *tao* in action. It mixes things but does not repress them. It focuses on the way and the power that is common to all. Don't be fluid and versatile. Establish principles and boundaries that endure. Persevering endures over time. The solid is above, the flexible is below. Thunder and wind work together to ground things and stir them up to new growth. What is solid and what is supple are completely in harmony. Putting your ideas to the trial brings profit and insight. Endure in the way. The way of heaven and earth endures without coming to an end. Imposing a direction or having a place to go brings profit and insight. When you complete something let it become the beginning of the new. The sun and the moon have heaven, and thus their light endures. The four seasons transform and change, and thus they enable lasting accomplishment. The wise person endures in the way, and thus the human world changes and perfects itself. Contemplate where you persevere. By doing so you can see the deep purpose of all the myriad beings.

Transforming Lines

Initial six: Deepening persevering. You are going too deep, too soon. This will cut you off from the spirits and leave you open to danger. Don't try to impose a direction on things. There is nothing you can do that would be advantageous. *Direction:* Let the situation grow and mature. The strength is there. Be resolute. You are connected to a creative force.

Nine at-second: Take action. All your regrets will be extinguished. This brings lasting ability, power and skill. Stay in the centre. *Direction:* Be very careful at the beginning. Don't be afraid to act alone. You are connected to a creative force.

Nine at-third: Not persevering your power to realize *tao*. If you receive gifts or commands, you will only be embarrassed. Putting your ideas to the trial brings the shame and regret of having lost the way. There is nothing that can help you here. *Direction:* Release bound energy. Deliver yourself from the problem. The situation is already changing.

Nine at-fourth: There is no game in these fields. Under no conditions should you endure in this situation! Slip away quietly and acquire what you need. *Direction:* Make the effort. If you let yourself be led, you can realize your hidden potential. The situation is already changing.

Six at-fifth: You must choose if you will persevere in this situation. If you wish to act like a wife, or are in the female tradition, continuing on will generate meaning and good fortune by releasing transformative energy. If you wish to act like a husband or a son, in the male tradition, continuing on cuts you off from the spirits and leaves you open to danger. You must choose. If you choose the wife, adhere to this one thing and follow it through. If you choose the husband and son, cut yourself off from this situation to preserve your integrity. By staying you would be cut off from the spirits and left open to danger. *Direction:* This is a time of transition. Don't be afraid to act alone. You are connected to a creative force.

Six above: Rousing persevering. Too much excitement and agitation. If you go on like this, you will be cut off from the spirits and left open to danger. If a commander acts like this, nothing can be achieved. *Direction:* Find an image for what is bothering you and cook it in the imaginative vessel. Be resolute about this. It will connect you to a creative force.

33 Retiring,
TUN

Keywords: Withdraw, conceal yourself, be small, be happy.

Retiring describes your situation in terms of conflict and withdrawal. The way to deal with it is to pull back and seclude yourself in order to prepare for a better time. This is pleasing to the spirits. Through it they will give you success, power and the capacity to bring the situation to maturity. Putting your ideas to the trial brings profit and insight. Don't impose yourself on the world. Be small. Adapt to whatever crosses your path.

> **Retire,** TUN: Withdraw, run away, escape, flee, hide yourself; disappear, withdraw into obscurity, become invisible; secluded, anti-social; fool or trick someone. The ideogram portrays a pig (the sign of wealth and good fortune) and the sign for walk away. It suggests satisfaction, luck and wealth through withdrawing.

The hexagram figure shows an inner limit that connects with the spirit above. Below heaven, the mountain. Retire and be coupled with heaven. You can't stay where you are. Withdraw, pull back, decline involvements, refuse connections. Keep people who busily seek their own advantage at a distance, not through hate but through a demanding severity that inspires fear and awe. Retiring is pleasing to the spirits. It is solid, appropriate and corresponds to the movement of the time. Putting your ideas to the trial brings profit and insight. Be small, adaptable and flexible. Immerse yourself in the situation and endure. Knowing when to retire is a great and righteous thing!

Transforming Lines

Initial six: Retiring's tail. You are caught and held fast. Difficulties. You are confronting an angry old ghost who returns to take revenge for past mistreatment. It is no use to impose a direction on things or to have a place to go. Stay where you are and avoid calamity. *Direction:* Find a supportive group. Stay inside it. You are coupled with a creative force.

Six at-second: Stubbornly bind yourself to this plan. Don't let anything succeed in prying you loose. Make your purpose firm, then move with it out of danger. *Direction:* You are coupled with a creative force.

Nine at-third: Tied retiring. You are afflicted and endangered through your connection with others. There is an angry ghost here, who has returned to take revenge for past mistreatment. You can't deal with this situation directly. Gather servants, who can help you communicate with the authorities and carry out your plans, and concubines, who can deflect enemies and create a pleasing atmosphere. This is an exhausting and wearisome situation. You will not be able to achieve anything great. *Direction:* Communication is blocked. Proceed step by step. Gather energy for a decisive new move.

Nine at-fourth: Pleasurable retiring. Pleasure, affection, beauty and order lead and are led into retiring. This generates meaning and good fortune by releasing transformative energy. Use the oracle to stay in touch with the *tao*. Don't be adaptable. Don't talk to unimportant people. That will only obstruct things now. *Direction:* Proceed step by step. Gather energy for a decisive new move.

Nine at-fifth: Excellence retiring. What is fine, intelligent, gives pleasure and happiness leads and is led into retiring. Putting your ideas to the trial generates meaning and good fortune by releasing transformative energy. Your purpose is correct. *Direction:* Continue the search on your own. Don't be afraid to stand alone. This is a time of transition. You are connected to a creative force.

Nine above: Fertile retiring. There is nothing for which this will not, ultimately, be advantageous. It ushers in a time of abundance. What is rich, fertilizing and abounding leads and is led into retiring. Have no doubts. *Direction:* This is a significant influence. It will couple you with a creative force.

34 Great Invigorating, TA CHUANG

  Keywords: Have a firm purpose. Focus your strength and go forward.

Great Invigorating describes your situation in terms of strength, drive and invigorating power. The way to deal with it is to focus your strength through a central creative idea. Putting your ideas to the trial will bring profit and insight. Beware of hurting others through excessive use of force.

Great, TA: Big, noble, important; able to protect others; orient your will towards a self-imposed goal; the ability to lead or guide your life; yang energy.

Invigorate, CHUANG: Inspire, animate, strengthen; strong, flourishing, robust; mature, in the prime of life (25 – 40 years old); *also:* Damage, wound, unrestrained use of strength. The ideogram portrays a robust man, stout and strong as a tree.

The hexagram figure shows inner force expressing itself directly and decisively. Thunder located above heaven. This is a time for resolute action. Come out of retirement. It is important to be able to hold on to your strength, for you must judge things for yourself and proceed on your own. A great idea implies strength and power. Something solid and strong is stirring things up. This is the source of your strength. Putting your ideas to the trial brings profit and insight. Correct onesidedness in yourself and others. Having a great idea and continually correcting your path lets you look into the heart of heaven and earth.

Transforming Lines

Initial nine: Invigorating strength in your feet. Hold back and accumulate energy. Things are just beginning. This is not a time to set out on an expedition or to discipline people. You would be cut off from the spirits and exposed to danger. Act with confidence, for you are linked to the spirits and they will carry you through. There is the danger of exhaustion if you act too quickly. *Direction:* Continue in the same direction. Be resolute. You are connected to a creative force.

Nine at-second: Put your plan to the trial. This generates meaning and good fortune by releasing transformative energy. Stay centred. *Direction:* This begins a time of great abundance. Don't be afraid to act alone. You are connected to a creative force.

Nine at-third: In this situation, only small people would try to push forward. Use the oracle to stay in touch with the *tao*. Don't use weapons. Be empty, like the empty spaces in a net. You are confronting an angry old ghost who has returned to take revenge for past mistreatment. If you charge ahead like a billy goat trying to butt his way through a hedge, you will only entangle your horns and lose your strength and power. Use a net, not a club. *Direction:* If you let yourself be led, you can realize your hidden potential. The situation is already moving.

Nine at-fourth: Put your plan to the trial. This generates meaning and good fortune by releasing transformative energy. All your regrets will disappear. The obstacle that entangles you will be broken up. Use your invigorating strength like the axles of a great cart. Bring things together and carry them forward. *Direction:* This begins a great and flourishing time. If you let yourself be led, you can realize your hidden potential. The situation is already changing.

Six at-fifth: You have lost your goats and sheep. Your property and thoughts vanish. Be versatile. Move with the sudden change. You will have no cause to regret it. Your current situation is not appropriate. *Direction:* Be resolute. You are connected to a creative force.

Six above: A billy goat tries to butt through the hedge. He can't pull back, and he can't break through. You are caught here. Imposing a direction or having a place to go will not help at all. You are in for a spell of drudgery. But this hard work will generate meaning and good fortune by releasing transformative energies. A lack of forethought got you stuck here, but the fault won't last for long. *Direction:* Your hard work can open a great new time. Be resolute. You are connected to a creative force.

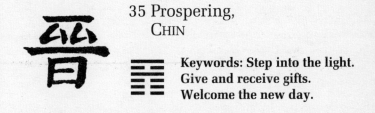

35 Prospering, CHIN

Keywords: Step into the light. Give and receive gifts. Welcome the new day.

Prospering describes your situation in terms of emerging slowly and surely into the full light of day. The way to deal with it is to give freely in order to help things emerge and flourish. Be calm in your strength and poise. Take delight in things. Give gifts of strength and spirit to enhance those connected with you. You will be received by the higher powers three times in a single day.

> **Prosper,** CHIN: Grow and flourish, as young plants do in the sun; advance, increase, progress; be promoted, rise, go up; permeate, impregnate. The ideogram portrays birds taking flight as the sun appears at dawn.

The hexagram figure shows light emerging from the covering earth. Brightness issues forth above the earth. The time has come to re-imagine the situation. Invigorating strength has carried you forward. This implies advancing, exerting yourself, furthering the development of things, stepping into the light. Use the source of this new light to brighten your own power to realize the *tao*. Prospering is a time to advance. Be yielding and join with others in order to brighten your own great idea. What is flexible and adaptable is advancing, and will move

111

you to the position above. Be calm in your strength and poise and give gifts of strength and spirit. You will be received by the higher powers three times in one day.

Transforming Lines

Initial six: In order to prosper, hold back at first. Putting your ideas to the trial generates meaning and good fortune by releasing transformative energy. But let emptiness carry you forward. Use a net and not a weapon. Act with confidence, for you are linked to the spirits and they will carry you through. Being generous is not a mistake. Take independent action to correct the situation. You have not yet received your mandate from fate. *Direction:* Bite through the obstacle. Re-imagine the situation. Gather your forces for a decisive new move.

Six at-second: In order to prosper, accept the sorrow and fear the situation brings. Put your ideas to the trial. This generates meaning and good fortune by releasing transformative energy. This is a constricting situation, but it brings great blessing from the queen and the mothers. Make correcting one-sidedness and error your central concern. *Direction:* Gather energy for a decisive new move.

Six at-third: The crowds have confidence in you. All cause to repent will be extinguished. People affirm your purpose. Move upwards. *Direction:* Leave your present situation. Don't be afraid to act alone. You are connected to a creative force.

Nine at-fourth: Prosperity brings bushy-tailed rodents, timid skulking animals that eat up stored grain. This indicates the presence of an angry old ghost who returns to take revenge for past mistreatment. Don't act on this idea. The situation is not appropriate. *Direction:* Strip away these old ideas. Be open to new ones. Don't take the lead. Provide what is needed.

Six at-fifth: Take action. All cause to repent will be extin-guished. Don't worry about gaining or losing. Have no cares. This will generate meaning and good fortune by releasing transformative energy. There is nothing for which this will not, ultimately, be advantageous. It can usher in a time of abundance. To go on will bring rewards. *Direction:* Be careful of who you associate with. Proceed step by step. Gather energy for a decisive new move.

Nine above: Use strength carefully. Deal with your own problems first. Confronting your ghosts, the angry spirits that return to seek revenge for past mistreatment, will generate meaning and good fortune by releasing transformative energy. This is not a mistake. Putting your ideas to the trial right now will only result in losing the right way; your way is not clear yet. *Direction:* Prepare for the call to action. Re-imagine the situation. Gather energy for a decisive new move.

36 Brightness Hiding, Ming Yi

**Keywords: Hide your light.
Accept the difficult task.**

Brightness Hiding describes your situation in terms of entering the darkness to protect yourself, or to begin a difficult new endeavour. The way to deal with it is to hide your light. Conceal your intelligence by voluntarily entering what is beneath you, like the sun as it sets in the evening. There is a real possibility of injury in the situation. By dimming the light of your awareness and entering the darkness you can avoid being hurt. You have the chance to release yourself from your problems and inaugurate a new time. Putting your ideas to the trial by accepting drudgery and difficulty will bring you profit and insight.

> **Brightness,** Ming: The light from fire, sun, moon and stars; consciousness, awareness, human intelligence, understanding; illuminate, distinguish clearly; lucid, clear, evident; *also:* A bright bird, the golden pheasant. The ideogram portrays the sun and the moon.

Hide, YI: Keep out of sight; distant, remote; raze, lower, level; ordinary, plain, colourless; cut, wound, destroy, exterminate; barbarians, strangers, vulgar, uncultured people. The ideogram portrays a threatening man armed with a bow.

The hexagram figure shows inner light hidden in common labour. Brightness enters the earth's centre. Deliverance from your problems is already being prepared, so accept what is confronting you. Advancing always creates the possibility of injury. Hiding implies injury. You are being proscribed and excluded. Carefully watch the desires that connect you with others so you can consciously choose when to darken or to brighten them. Brighten the pattern within yourself while yielding to outer darkness. Use the enveloping obscurity and the difficulties confronting you to clarify worthy ideas. Be like King Wen, who organized the *I Ching* when he was imprisoned by a tyrant. Accept drudgery and difficulty. This brings profit and insight. Darken your light, accept the inner heaviness and let it correct your purpose. Be like Prince Chi, who knew how to distinguish what is right in a difficult time and who became a model for others.

Transforming Lines

Initial nine: Hiding your brightness through flying. Though your wings are drooping, carry on with your flight. Use the oracle to stay in touch with the *tao*. Go on for three days without taking anything in. Impose a direction on things. Have a place to go. Master your words in order to persuade others of your authority. *Direction:* Stay humble and connected to basic facts. You can deliver yourself from this problem. The situation is already changing.

Six at-second: Hiding your brightness, you are wounded in the left thigh. This is a serious but not deadly wound. Don't let it stop you. Rescue yourself. Use the strength of a horse to ride away quickly. This generates meaning and good fortune by releasing transformative energy. Yield and work with the movement. *Direction:* A flourishing time is coming. If you let yourself be led, you can realize your hidden potential. The situation is already changing.

Nine at-third: Hide your brightness in the southern hunt. In the midst of difficulties you capture the great leader and take his head. Putting your ideas to the trial will free you from affliction, disorder and hatred. *Direction:* Something important is returning. Be open to it. Provide what is needed.

Six at-fourth: You enter the left belly and take the heart of the hiding brightness. Leave this place, this family, this way of thinking. You have captured the meaning, so don't be sorry. *Direction:* This begins a time of abundance. Don't be afraid to act alone. You are connected to a creative force.

Six at-fifth: Hide your brightness like Prince Chi. He continued in his position in a difficult time without losing his integrity. Don't pause in your efforts to clarify things. Putting your ideas to the trial brings profit and insight. *Direction:* The situation is already changing.

Nine above: This plan doesn't brighten things; it darkens things. At first it mounts to heaven, then it falls to earth. At first it illuminates the cities of the world, then everything is lost. This is position of the oppressive tyrant. Let go of this idea. *Direction:* The situation is corrupt. Deliver yourself from this desire. The situation is already changing.

37 Dwelling (Clan) People, CHIA JEN

Keywords: Hold together. Stay inside. Adapt, nourish, endure.

Dwelling People describes your situation in terms of living and working with others. The way to deal with it is to care for your relationship with the people who share your space and your activities. Take care of the dwelling and what is within it.

Profit and insight come through the woman and through a flexible, nourishing attitude. Dwell in the yin.

> **Dwell,** CHI: Home, house, household, family, relations, clan; a business; a school of thought; master of a skill or art; hold something in common with others. The ideogram portrays a roof over a pig or a dog, the most valued domestic animals.

> **People,** JEN: Human beings; an individual; humanity. The ideogram portrays a person kneeling in prayer or submission.

The hexagram figure shows warmth and clarity spreading within the dwelling. Wind originating from fire issues forth. Gather energy for a decisive new move. When you are injured in the outer world, you naturally turn back towards the dwelling. Dwelling people means what is inside. Use your words to connect with people and make your actions persevering. A woman's yin attitude can correct the situation inside; a man's yang attitude can correct the situation outside. Together they reflect the great righteousness of heaven and earth. The dwelling needs a strong head. The roles of father and mother should be clearly designated. Let whoever is the father be a father, the son be a son; let whoever is the elder be the elder, the younger be the younger. Let whoever is the husband be a husband, and whoever is the wife be a wife. This is the correct way of the dwelling. When you correct the dwelling, you set the world right.

Transforming Lines

Initial nine: Fences, barriers, bars on the doors are what define a dwelling. Stay inside it now. All your regrets will disappear. Your purpose hasn't transformed itself yet. *Direction:* Act step by step. Gather energy for a decisive new move.

Six at-second: Being without a direction, not having a place to go or imposing a direction on things, frees you to respond to what needs to be done. Dwell in the inner centre. Prepare the meals and the offerings. Acting in this way generates meaning and good fortune by releasing transformative energy. Yield and work with the movement. Penetrate to the core of the situation in order to ground your desires. *Direction:* Accumulate small things to acheive something great. Turn potential conflict into creative tension. The situation is already changing.

Nine at-third: Relentlessly scold the people in your dwelling. This is a difficult time. An angry old ghost has returned to seek revenge for past mistreatment. Confronting this spirit and repenting over past conduct generates meaning and good fortune by releasing transformative energy. If the wife and the children laugh and giggle at this, it will end in the humiliation of having lost the right way. If you let go of your demands and your severity, the dwelling will simply dissolve. *Direction:* Increase your efforts. A fertile time is coming. Strip away old ideas. Provide what is needed.

Six at-fourth: An affluent dwelling. Have a central idea. This generates great meaning and good fortune by releasing transformative energy. Yield and work with the movement. *Direction:* Bring people together. Take action. You are coupled with a creative force.

Nine at-fifth: A king imagines possessing a dwelling. What would it be like? A house full of spirits that could care for all the many beings. Have no cares and act from your heart. This generates meaning and good fortune by releasing transformative energy. Mingle with others in mutual affection. *Direction:* Adorn the house with beauty. Release bound energy. This will deliver you from your sorrows. The situation is already changing.

Nine above: Act on your plan with confidence. You are linked to the spirits and they will carry you through. You will impress everyone through this power. Carrying your plan to completion generates meaning and good fortune by releasing transformative energy. You have the impressive power of the spirits behind you. You can acquire significance and completely reverse the way you are regarded. *Direction:* The situation is already changing.

38 Polarizing,
K'UEI

Keywords: Change conflict into creative tension through awareness.

Polarizing describes your situation in terms of opposition and discord. The way to deal with it is to change potential conflict into dynamic tension. Separate and clarify what is in conflict while acknowledging the essential connection. Small things are important now. Be flexible and adaptable in all your affairs. That generates meaning and good fortune by releasing transformative energy. Be open to strange occurrences, sudden visions and non-normal ways of seeing things.

> **Polarize,** KUEI: Oppose, separate, create distance; different, discordant; antagonistic, contrary, mutually exclusive; creative tension; at the opposite ends of an axis, 180° apart; astronomical or polar opposition; squint, look at things from an unusual perspective; strange, weird.

The hexagram figure shows expression and awareness in conflict with each other. Fire rises, the mists descend. The solution to this conflict is inherent in the situation. When the way of dwelling together is exhausted, you must necessarily turn away. Polarizing implies turning away. It is what is outside, what is unfamiliar, foreign and strange. You must be able to both join things together and to separate them. Fire stirs things up and rises. The mists stir things up and descend. They are like two women who agree to live together while their purposes move apart. These two things, individual expression and holding together, can be connected through brightness and awareness. Use what is flexible and adaptable to move to the position above. You can acquire the centre and connect with what is strong and solid. That is why being concerned with small things generates meaning and good fortune by releasing transformative energy. Heaven and earth are polarized, but in their work they come together. Man and woman are polarized, but their purposes interpenetrate. The myriad beings are polarized, but they all are busy with the same things. Examine what separates and what connects people. Polarizing is a time when you can connect with what is truly great.

Transforming Lines

Initial nine: Don't worry. All your regrets will disappear. Even though you have lost your horse, don't pursue it. Your spirit, strength and property will return of themselves because they belong to you. When you see hateful people, don't get entangled in their twisted emotions. Cast the harm and error out of yourself. *Direction:* Gather energy for a decisive new move.

Nine at-second: You meet a lord in a narrow street, a place between things. This is someone important who can help and teach you. The meeting is not a mistake. You have not let go of the *tao* in this encounter. *Direction:* Bite through the obstacles. Gather energy for a decisive new move.

Six at-third: You see a cart being dragged back. The cattle pulling it are hindered and hobbled. The people accompanying it have their heads shaved and their noses cut off. All are punished by losing public face and honour. Initially, you will not be able to carry your plan to completion. The situation is not appropriate. You will unexpectedly encounter solid opposition. *Direction:* If you want to go through with this, you must clarify and brighten your central idea. Be resolute. You are connected to a creative force.

Nine at-fourth: The conflict has cut you off. You are alone, like an orphan without a protector, and must originate yourself. You unexpectedly meet a powerful being, a source of good fortune and benevolent care. Join this being with confidence. The spirits are with you and will carry you through. An angry old ghost has returned to take revenge for past mistreatment. Go through the difficulties. This is not a mistake. Your purpose is moving. *Direction:* Decrease your present involvements to make energy available for new ones. Curb your anger. This is the return of something significant. Don't take the lead. Provide what is needed.

Six at-fifth: Take action. All your regrets will disappear. Your ancestor is gnawing through the flesh to find you. An old connection returns. Partake of the sacrifice that links you with friends and ancestral spirits. How could it be a mistake to proceed like this? It will bring rewards. *Direction:* Go your way step by step. Find a supportive group. Stay inside it. Gather energy for a decisive new move.

Nine above: The conflict has cut you off. You are alone, like an orphan without a protector, and must originate yourself. You see pigs carrying mud on their backs. Is this how the people around you are acting? Collect yourself. Gather all your souls into one vehicle. At first you will draw the bow to defend against attack, then you will unbend it in relaxation and friendship. Don't treat those who are approaching you as outlaws. Seek alliances and marriages. As you go on your way, you will meet the rain, falling fast and furious. This generates meaning and good fortune by releasing transformative energy. The flock of doubts will be extinguished. *Direction:* If you let yourself be led, you can realize your hidden potential. The situation is already changing.

39 Limping / Difficulties, CHIEN

Keywords: Don't act.
Re-imagine the situation.

Limping describes your situation in terms of confronting obstacles and feeling afflicted by them. The way to deal with it is to see through the situation in a new way and gather energy for a decisive new move. Don't magnify your problems. You are limping along and your circulation is impeded. Retreat and join with others in view of future gains. That brings profit and insight. Attack, lonely efforts and dwelling on the past won't help at all. See great people. Contact important people who can help you and think about what your central idea really is.

Putting your ideas to the trial generates meaning and good fortune by releasing transformative energy.

> **Limping/Difficulties,** CHIEN: Walk lamely, proceed haltingly; difficulties, obstacles, obstructions; the feeling of being afflicted, unhappy and suffering; crooked, feeble, weak; poverty; pride. The ideogram portrays cold feet and impeded circulation.

The hexagram figure shows an inner limit and an outer danger. Above the mountain is the gorge. Gather your energy for a decisive new move. Turning away from something is always arduous and heavy. Limping implies heaviness. But by reversing the direction of what you are doing, you can renovate your power to realize the *tao*. This is a difficult and heavy time. There is danger in front of you; if you can see it and stop, you will really understand the situation. In a difficult time, retreating and joining with others brings profit and insight. You can acquire the strong, calm centre. Through attack and lonely striving you will only exhaust your *tao*. See great people. Consult those who can help you to see what is great in your own ideas. This brings profit and insight. Proceeding in this way leads to achievement. The situation is appropriate. Putting your ideas to the trial generates meaning and good fortune by releasing transformative energy. Correct the way you are apportioning power and who you depend on. By re-imagining your situation, you connect with what is truly great.

Transforming Lines

Initial six: If you try to push on, you will only be limping. If you come back, you meet with praise. The time of difficulty is going, a time of praise is coming. The proper thing to do is to wait for it. *Direction:* The situation is already changing.

Six at-second: A king's servant limps on, encountering difficulty after difficulty. He is in no way the source of the trouble. If you are in this position, forced to struggle on through no fault of your own, bring things to completion as simply as you can. *Direction:* Communicate with others on the level of your common needs. Turn potential conflict into creative tension. The situation is already changing.

Nine at-third: If you try to push on, you will only be limping. If you come back, the situation will be reversed. The time of difficulty is going, the coming time will reverse it. Stay inside. You will soon have cause to rejoice. *Direction:* Change who you are associating with. Strip away your old ideas. Be open to what is coming. Don't take the lead.

Six at-fourth: If you try to push on, you will only be limping. If you come back, you meet connection and continuity. The time of difficulty is going, the coming time will connect you to new events. The situation is appropriate. What is coming has real value. *Direction:* Open yourself to this influence. It will couple you to a creative force.

Nine at-fifth: In great difficulties, limping along with your idea, you meet friends and partners who join with you for profit and enjoyment. A time of mutual activity is coming. Make articulating these connections the centre of your concerns. *Direction:* Keep your words humble and connected. Release bound energy. The obstacles will dissolve. The situation is already changing.

Six above: If you try to push on, you will only be limping. If you come back, you meet greatness and eminence. The time of difficulty is going, the coming time will be ripe and full. It generates meaning and good fortune by releasing transformative energy. See great people. Consult those who can help you to see what is great in your own ideas. This brings profit and insight. Firmly locate your purpose inside yourself, and hold on to what you feel is valuable. *Direction:* Proceed step by step. Gather energy for a decisive new move.

40 Loosening / Deliverance, HSIEH

Keywords: Solve problems, untie knots, release blocked energy.

Loosening/Deliverance describes your situation in terms of a release from tension and the new energy that it makes available. The way to deal with it is to untie knots, dispel sorrows, solve problems and understand motivations. Forgive and forget, wipe the slate clean. Join with others to realize plans for future gain. That brings profit and insight. If you have no unfinished business to attend to, simply wait for the energy to return. It will generate meaning and good fortune. If you do have directions to impose or places to go, the first light of dawn generates meaning and good fortune by releasing transformative energy. Be up and doing and greet the new day.

> **Loosening/Deliverance,** HSIEH: Divide, detach, untie, scatter, sever, dissolve, dispel; analyse, explain, understand; free from constraint, dispel sorrow, eliminate effects, solve problems; discharge, get rid of; take care of needs. The ideogram portrays a sharp instrument made of horn, used to loosen knots.

The hexagram figure shows the fertile shock of a stirring new time. Thunder and rain arousing. The situation is already changing. The time can't always be heavy and arduous. Deliverance implies relaxing and letting things go. Forgive excesses, pardon violations and faults. Act to stir things up. Loosening means arousing things and avoiding danger. Join with others to realize plans for future gain. That brings profit and insight. By going on you will acquire the crowds. The returning energy that is coming towards you will generate meaning and good fortune. Use it to stay in the centre. If you have places to go or directions to impose, the first light of dawn generates meaning and good fortune by releasing transformative energy. Proceeding in this way brings achievement. Heaven and earth loosen and free things through the arousing power of thunder and rain. Thunder and rain arouse the seeds of all the fruits, grasses and trees to burst forth. The time of loosening and deliverance is a great time indeed.

Transforming Lines

Initial six: Act on your plan. There is no harm or error in your situation. You are right at the border, the point of emergence. This position is proper and just. *Direction:* If you let yourself be led, you can realize your hidden potential. The situation is already changing.

Nine at-second: While hunting in the fields, you catch three foxes and acquire a yellow arrow. This is an omen of power. You eliminate three crafty enemies. You acquire the power of the foxes to change shape and move in the night-world. You learn to direct your force through connection to the earth and the centre. Put your ideas to the trial. This generates meaning and good fortune by releasing transformative energy. Stay in the centre and move with the *tao. Direction:* Gather strength so you can respond when the call to action comes. Re-imagine the situation. Gather energy for a decisive new move.

Six at-third: You are carrying things on your back and, at the same time, riding in a coach. These two things do not go together. One way or another, you are not in your place. This will end by attracting outlaws and robbers. Putting your ideas to the trial will only result in regrets and humiliation. Deliver yourself from this shameful situation. You are attracting the danger. The fault lies with you. Get rid of it. *Direction:* Endure in what is right, no matter what the cost. Be resolute. Take action. The change will connect you with a creative force.

Nine at-fourth: Loosen your thumbs, untie your big toes. You are bound too tightly to grasp things or walk. Split things apart. Bring partnerships to an end. Act this way with confidence, for you are connected to the spirits and they will carry you through. Your situation is not yet appropriate. *Direction:* Organize your forces. Something significant is returning. Be open to the new. Provide what is needed.

Six at-fifth: Use the oracle to stay in touch with the *tao*. You are held fast in the present situation, but you can find ways to loosen things and deliver yourself. This generates meaning and good fortune by releasing transformative energy. Have confidence. You are connected to the spirits and they will carry you through. Be flexible and adapt to what crosses your path. This lets you withdraw from the situation. *Direction:* Look within and find a way to break out of this isolation. Find a supportive group. Stay inside it. Gather energy for a decisive new move.

Six above: A prince shoots at a hawk sitting on the high rampart above. He catches it. There is nothing for which this will not, ultimately, be advantageous. You can capture a rebellious opposing force and dissolve a perverse influence. *Direction:* Gather energy for a decisive new move.

41 Diminishing,
SUN

Keywords: Diminish yourself, decrease your involvements.

Diminishing describes your situation in terms of loss, sacrifice and the need for concentration. The way to deal with it is to decrease your involvements and free yourself from emotional entanglements. This makes energy available for new developments. Act this way with confidence, for you are connected to the spirits and they will carry you through. This is the origin of great good fortune and meaningful events. It is not a mistake. This is an enabling divination. Put your ideas to the trial. Have a place to go. Impose a direction on things. That brings profit and insight. Inquire into motivations; ask yourself why you are doing things. Use two ceremonial vessels to present your results to the spirits.

Diminish, SUN: Lessen, take away from, make smaller; weaken, humble; damage, lose, spoil, hurt; blame, criticize; offer in sacrifice, give up, give away; let things settle;

125

concentrate. The ideogram portrays a hand holding a ceremonial vessel, making an offering to the spirits.

The hexagram figure shows an outer limit that brings inner development to expression. Below the mountain there are the mists. Go back and start over. Something significant is returning. To release blocked energy, you must have a way to let things go. Diminishing is the way, for decreasing is the beginning of increasing. This is the way you adjust and repair your power to realize the *tao*. Diminishing is heavy and arduous at first, but it lets you be versatile and change with the time. It keeps harm at a distance. Curb your anger and resentment in order to block passions and desires. This changes the flow of energy. Diminish what is below and augment what is above. Your *tao* is moving in what is above. Diminish things with confidence, for you are connected to the spirits and they will carry you through. This is the origin of great good fortune and meaningful events. It is not a mistake. This is an enabling divination, so put your ideas to the trial. Inquire into motivations, particularly your own. Use two ceremonial vessels to present your results to the spirits. These two vessels correspond to the time. They are: diminishing what is strong and solid and augmenting what is supple and adaptable. This is in accord with the time. It fills what is empty. It connects you to the time so you can accompany it as it moves.

Transforming Lines

Initial nine: Bring this affair to a close and leave quickly. This is not a mistake. Reflect on and discuss what diminishing can bring. Have a noble purpose. *Direction:* There are things you are not yet aware of. The spirit is returning. Don't take the lead. Be open to the new.

Nine at-second: Put your ideas to the trial. This will bring profit and insight. Don't discipline and punish people or set out on an expedition. You will be cut off from the spirits and left open to danger. There is nothing that will be diminished by this plan. Everything will be augmented. *Direction:* Take the situation in. Nourish things. Provide what is needed.

Six at-third: When three people move together they will be diminished by one. When one person is moving, a friend will come. This is a time to go in twos. If you are lonely, have no doubts, the friend will come. If you are part of a group, think about how you will soon be diminished. *Direction:* The time is opening for great new endeavours. If you let yourself be led, you can realize your hidden potential. The situation is already changing.

Six at-fourth: Your affliction, sickness or hatred will be diminished by doing what you are contemplating. Send the message quickly. Spread your commands. This brings happiness and joy. It is not a mistake. It is truly a cause for rejoicing. *Direction:* Turn potential conflicts into creative tensions. The situation is already changing.

Six at-fifth: If you added ten coupled divinations with the tortoise shell oracle not a single one would contradict your plan! It would be hard to get a more favourable answer to your question. It is the source of great good fortune and meaningful events. The origin is shielded and protected by the spirits above. *Direction:* Bring your inner and outer circumstances into accord. You are truly connected. Nourish things. Provide what is needed.

Nine above: Nothing will be diminished by this plan. Everything will be augmented. This is not a mistake. Putting your ideas to the trial will generate meaning and good fortune by releasing transformative energy. Have a place to go. Impose a direction on things. That brings profit and insight. You will obtain people to help you but not a dwelling place. Your purpose can make great gains. *Direction:* A significant connection is approaching. Return to meet it. Provide what is needed. Be open to the new.

42 Augmenting, YI

**Keywords: A fertile time.
Expand, increase, pour in more.**

Augmenting describes your situation in terms of increase, advance and development. The way to deal with it is to increase your involvements and pour in more energy. This is a time of gain, profit and expansion. Have a place to go. Impose a direction on things. Enter the stream of life with a purpose or embark on a significant enterprise. These things bring profit and insight.

> **Augment,** YI: Increase, advance, add to; benefit, strengthen, support; pour in more, superabundant, overflowing; restorative, fertile; useful, profitable, advantageous. The ideogram portrays a vessel overflowing with material and spiritual benefits.

The hexagram figure shows arousing new energy penetrating the outer world. Wind and thunder augmenting. Strip away your old ideas. By continually diminishing things, you have created augmenting, for increase and decrease are each other's beginning. Through augmenting you enrich your power to realize the *tao*. Augmenting continually enriches things without setting up structures. It uses flourishing and harvesting. When you can imagine improvement, shift the way you do things. When there is excess or error, correct it. Diminish what is above and augment what is below. Stimulate people at their work without limiting them. The source above has descended, and its *tao* is shining greatly. Let it stimulate you. Having a place to go or imposing a direction on things brings profit and insight. Make correcting one-sidedness and error the centre of your concerns. It will bring rewards. Entering the stream of life with a purpose or embarking on significant enterprises brings profit and insight. Secure your vehicle, the boat to carry you, then make your move. Augmenting stirs things up and grounds them. Like the sun rising, it has no limits. When heaven spreads out, earth gives birth. Together they increase and augment things on all sides. Augment everything. This connects you with the time, so you can accompany it as it moves.

Transforming Lines

Initial nine: Activate your ideas and rouse yourself to begin great efforts. This brings profit and insight. It is the origin of great good fortune and meaningful events. This is not a mistake, even though you are below in this situation and your resources are not great. *Direction:* Contemplate the field of action. Let everything come into view. Strip away old ideas. Be open to what is coming. Provide what is needed.

Six at-second: If you added ten coupled divinations with the tortoise-shell oracle not a single one would contradict your plan! It would be hard to get a more favourable answer to your question. Putting your ideas to the trial will be a perpetual source of great good fortune and meaningful events. Be like the king presenting a sacrifice to the supreme powers. Use your idea to create meaning and good fortune for all. You are the source of effective power. What augments you comes from the outside, and it is indeed on its way. *Direction:* Bring your inner and outer circumstances into accord. You are truly connected. Nourish things. Provide what is needed.

Six at-third: You can be augmented through making use of unfortunate events when everyone else seems stuck in a pit. This is not a mistake. Act with confidence, for you are connected to the spirits and they will carry you through. The centre of things is moving. Notify the authorities and connect the movement with your basic principles. Use your right to speak. Take a firm grip on things. *Direction:* Find a supportive group. Stay inside it. Gather energy for a decisive new move.

Six at-fourth: The centre of things is moving. Notify the authorities and connect the movement with your basic principles. Actively involve yourself in this shift of the centre of activity. This brings profit and insight. By connecting with it you augment your own purpose. *Direction:* Stay out of quarrels and emotional nastiness. Proceed step by step. Gather energy for a decisive new move.

Nine at-fifth: Take action. You are connected to the spirits and they will carry you through. Have confidence. Act with a benevolent heart. There is no question that this will be the source of great good fortune and meaningful events. The spirits will carry you through. Benevolence is your personal key to realizing the *tao*. Do not question it in any way. Your purpose will make great gains. *Direction:* Take things in. Provide what is needed.

Nine above: This plan brings absolutely no augmenting. It is dangerous and will leave you open to attack. You have not given your heart an enduring foundation. By acting this way you cut yourself off from the spirits and leave yourself open to danger. You are acting on one-sided evidence. If you go on, you will attract attack from outside. *Direction:* Articulate your limits. Strip away your old ideas. Be open to the new. Don't take the lead.

43 Resolution / Parting, KUAI

Keywords: Decide and act resolutely. Clean it out and bring it to light.

Resolution/Parting describes your situation in terms of resolutely confronting difficulties. The way to deal with it is to clarify what you must do and act on it, even if you must leave something behind. Display your decision resolutely at the centre of effective power. Have confidence in proclaiming it, for you are connected to the spirits and they will carry you through. You will confront difficulties. There is an angry old ghost in the situation who has returned to take revenge for past mistreatment. Notify those who love, trust and depend on you. Don't resort to arms, attack or build up defences. Have a place to go. Impose a direction on things. That brings profit and insight.

> **Resolution/Parting,** KUAI: Decide, declare, resolve on; resolute, prompt, decisive, stern; certain, settled; open and cleanse a wound; water opening a path through a barrier; *also:* Separate, fork, cut off; flow in different directions.

The hexagram figure shows inner force coming to expression. The mists rise above heaven. Act with drive and persistence. By continually augmenting things you break through obstacles. Resolution implies breaking through. What is solid and strong breaks through and breaks up what is supple and adaptable. Spread your wealth so you can depend on what is below you. Concern yourself with realizing the *tao* and keep out of other activities. This is a time to break through. Persist in your efforts to express things. Break through the obstacles to harmony. Display your resolution in the centre of power. Though you may be small, five strong forces are behind you. Have confidence. The spirits will give you the power to express yourself. Although you must confront difficulties, this exposure to danger will make you shine. Notify those who depend on you. Don't resort to arms. If you do you will exhaust all chance of honour and eminence. Have a place to go. Impose a direction on things. That brings profit and insight. What is strong and solid endures. Bring your plan to completion.

Transforming Lines

Initial nine: There is invigorating strength in the foot behind you. Think about this move before you pick your foot up and take the first step. This is not the way to activate things. Your stance is faulty. If you proceed like this, you will not overcome the difficulties. *Direction:* Don't be afraid to act alone. You are connected to a creative force.

Nine at-second: Alarms and outcries. A tense situation. You must be on guard day and night. Have no cares. You will acquire what you want. Your *tao* flows in the centre. *Direction:*

This brings revolution and renewal. Change the way you present yourself. You are coupled with a creative force.

Nine at-third: There is invigorating strength in the cheek-bones. These are cruel people who insist on their mastery. By associating with them, you will be cut off from the spirits and left open to danger. Use the oracle to stay in touch with the *tao*. Resolutely leave this situation. Going on alone, you will be caught in the rain, soaked and polluted. Your feeling of indignation at how you have been treated is not a mistake. Part from these people! Bringing your connection to an end is not a mistake. *Direction:* Express your feelings. Find a supportive group. Stay inside it. The situation is already changing.

Nine at-fourth: Buttocks without flesh and you are moving your camp. Hurt, flayed or punished, you are moving on, dragged like a goat on a leash. Don't lose your capacity to act directly. Your doubts and regrets will soon be extinguished. If you hear someone telling you what to believe, don't trust them. The situation is not appropriate. Your understanding will not be brightened by this talk. *Direction:* Wait for the right moment to act. Turn potential conflict into creative tension. The situation is already changing.

Nine at-fifth: A bunch of abundantly proliferating weeds calls for extremely resolute action. If you want to deal with this problem, you must get to the centre and pull it up in all its ramifications. This is not a mistake. Because it is hidden in the swampy growth, your own centre is not shining yet. *Direction:* Invigorate your central idea. Be resolute. You are connected to a creative force.

Six above: Don't go on without crying out or communicating. It will cut you off from the spirits and leave you open to danger. You won't live long that way. Call out! Communicate! *Direction:* Take action. You are connected to a creative force.

44 Welcoming / Coupling, Kou

Keywords: Welcome it, then let it go. Trust what the experience brings.

Welcoming/Coupling describes your situation in terms of opening yourself to welcome what comes. You can deal with it by realizing that the brief and intense moment of encounter reflects a connection of the primal powers. Don't try to control it. The connection is there, even if it seems accidental. The woman and the yin are full of invigorating strength. Don't try to grasp and hold on to things. What seems a brief contact connects you with a creative force.

Welcoming/Coupling, Kou: Meet, encounter, open yourself to; find something or someone on your path; the encounter of the primal powers, yin and yang; copulate, all forms of sexual intercourse; magnetism, gravity, mating of animals, gripped by impersonal forces; fortuitous; favourable, good. The ideogram portrays sexual intercourse.

The hexagram figure shows the spirit spreading throughout the world. Below heaven there is wind. You are coupled with a creative force. Coupling implies unexpected encounters, lucky coincidences, enjoyable happenings. What is supple and what is solid are meeting. Queens and kings use this time to spread their mandates to the four corners of the world. This a time of meetings. Don't grasp and hold on to things. The time does not permit these contacts to endure. Heaven and earth meet each other and all the different kinds of beings join together in beautiful display. What is solid and strong meets what is central and correct. The great is moving below heaven. The time of welcoming and coupling is truly and righteously great!

Transforming Lines

Initial six: Attached to a metal chock, this cart can't go forward. Movement is stopped so that you can investigate things. Put your ideas to the trial. This generates meaning and good fortune by releasing transformative energy. Have a place to go. Impose a direction on things. First try to visualize where you could be trapped and cut off from the spirits. There is an emaciated pig entangled in this situation. Something is interfering with the flow of wealth, good fortune and enjoyment. If you can find out why this pig is dragging its lame hoof, it will connect you to the spirits and carry you through. Let yourself be drawn by the supple and adaptable. *Direction:* Take action. You are connected to a creative force.

Nine at-second: There are fish in this enclosure. It is a womb pregnant with coming abundance. There is no harm or error in this situation. Don't invite guests and don't visit others. Don't extend yourself. *Direction:* Retire and nourish the growing creative force.

Nine at-third: Buttocks without flesh and you are moving your camp. Hurt, flayed or punished, you are moving on. You confront an angry ghost who has returned to take revenge for past mistreatment. This is dangerous. If you can find a central idea to organize yourself, you will make no great mistake. Take independent action. Move of your own free will, don't be dragged along. *Direction:* Firmly and convincingly state your case. Find a supportive group. Gather energy for a decisive new move.

Nine at-fourth: This enclosure has no fish; a sterile womb. Don't count on this to undertake anything. You will be cut off from the spirits and left open to danger. You are too far from your underlying support. *Direction:* Gently penetrate to the core of the situation. Turn potential conflict into creative tension. The situation is already changing.

Nine at-fifth: Weaving willow branches to enclose melons, symbols of heaven and earth. A containing elegance tumbles down from its source in heaven. The pliant strands of your composition contain the cosmos, revealing a hidden magic. Whether this is something you are making, or chapters in the book of life, it indicates a wonderful and creative time. Stay centred and correct. Don't set aside heaven's mandate. Make it one with your purpose. *Direction:* Transform the world into imagination. Be resolute. You are connected to a creative force.

Nine above: Coupling with your horns, a trial of strength. This brings shame and regrets, though no serious harm. Being on top will exhaust and humiliate you. *Direction:* Don't be afraid to act alone. You can contact a creative force.

45 Clustering, TS'UI

Keywords: Gather, assemble, animate. A great effort brings great rewards.

Clustering describes your situation in terms of collecting and gathering. The way to deal with it is to unite people and things through a common feeling or goal. Concentrate the crowd and turn it into an organized whole. This is pleasing to the spirits. Through it they will give you success, effective power and the capacity to bring the situation to maturity. This is the time for great projects. Be like the king who imagines a temple full of images that unite people and connect them with greater forces. See great people. Visit those who can help and advise you. Look at your own central idea and how you organize your thoughts. This is pleasing to the spirits. Through it they will give you success, effective power and the capacity to bring the situation to maturity. Making a great offering to the spirit of this time generates meaning and good fortune by releasing transformative energy. Put your ideas to the trial. Have a place to go. Impose a direction on things. This brings profit and insight.

Cluster, T'SUI: Gather, call or pack together; tight groups of people, animals and things; assemble, concentrate, collect; reunite, reassemble; crowd, multitude, bunch; dense clumps of grass. The ideogram portrays a bunch of grass and a servant. It suggests gathering the capacity to do things.

The hexagram figure shows common labour coming to expression. The mists rise over the earth. Proceed step by step. First things meet in pairs, then they assemble. Clustering means assembling and reuniting. Eliminate the need for fighting and weapons by being alert. Don't be taken by surprise. Clustering implies collecting people together. Labour is its expression. The strong is in the centre and things will correspond to it. This is the source of assembling. Be like the king who imagines having a temple. This involves reverence and presenting things as offerings. See great people and think about your central idea. This allows you to correct how things come together. Making a great sacrifice generates meaning and good fortune by releasing transformative energy. Having a place to go and imposing a direction on things brings profit and insight. Yield and work with the heavenly mandate. By contemplating the place where people come together, you can look at the motives of heaven, earth and the myriad beings.

Transforming Lines

Initial six: Act with confidence. You are connected to the spirits and they will carry you through. At first you will not be able to bring your plan to completion. Things will be thrown into disorder. Bring them together again. Call out. One small effort, a handful, a handshake, triggers joy and laughter. Have no cares. Going on like this is not a mistake, even if your purpose is disarrayed. *Direction:* Follow the stream of events. Proceed step by step. Gather energy for a decisive new move.

Six at-second: Draw things out, prolong the time. This generates meaning and good fortune by releasing transformative energy. Let yourself be pulled in. Wait until you feel connected to the spirits involved, then proceed with your plan. Make an offering, even if your resources are thin. Gather energy in the centre. The situation isn't ready to change yet. *Direction:* Look within. Find a way to break out of the isolation. Find a supportive group. Gather energy for a decisive new move.

Six at-third: As soon as there is clustering, there is sorrow and mourning over painful recollections. Having a place to go or imposing a direction on things brings no advantage here. Move on. This is not a mistake. If you try to adapt to the situation, you will only be humiliated. Model yourself on something above you. *Direction:* Be open to a new influence. It will couple you with a creative force.

Nine at-fourth: Take action. Your plan will generate great good fortune and meaningful events by releasing transformative energy. It is not a mistake. This situation is not appropriate. *Direction:* Change who you are associating with. Strip away old ideas and be open to new ones. Provide what is needed.

Nine at-fifth: This is a cluster of people arranged according to rank. There is no connection to the spirits whatsoever in this group. This is not your fault. Try to find it. Search for the connection to the source again and again. This will extinguish your regrets. The purpose of the group is not clear yet. *Direction:* Gather strength so you act when the call to action comes. Re-imagine the situation. Gather energy for a decisive new move.

Six above: You are paying for this connection with sighs, tears and sniffles. It is not a question of blame. Though you are at the top, the house is not tranquil. You are surrounded by the wrong people. *Direction:* Communication is obstructed. You are connected to the wrong people. Proceed step by step. Gather energy for a decisive new move.

46 Ascending, SHENG

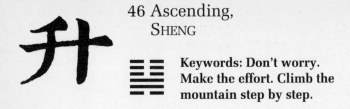

**Keywords: Don't worry.
Make the effort. Climb the
mountain step by step.**

Ascending describes your situation in terms of rising to a higher level and getting something done. The way to deal with it is set a goal and work towards it step by step. Root yourself and push towards the heights. Climb the mountain and connect with the spirits. Bring out and fulfil the hidden potential. This is a very favourable situation. It is pleasing to the spirits. It is the origin of growth, effective power and the capacity to bring things to maturity. See great people, those who can help and advise you. Look at the great in yourself and how you organize your ideas. Have no cares, fears or anxiety. Set out towards the south, the region of summer, growth, intensity and action. This generates meaning and good fortune by releasing transformative energy. Correct, discipline and put things in order.

Ascend, SHENG: Mount, go up, rise; climb step by step; advance through your own efforts; be promoted, rise in office; accumulate, bring out and fulfil the potential; distil liquor; an ancient standard of measure, a small cupful.

The hexagram figure shows inner adaptability rising from its roots in the earth. Earth's centre gives birth to the trees. If you let yourself be led, you can realize your hidden potential. When people assemble and set a higher goal, they call it ascending. It doesn't simply come to you. Yield to the impulse and work hard to realize the *tao*. Amass small things to reach what is high and great. Be supple and adaptable and use this time. Penetrate to the core. Adapt and work hard to yield results. What is strong is at the centre and things will correspond to it. This is pleasing to the great spirits. Through it they will give you success, effective power and the capacity to bring the situation to maturity. It will connect you to great people and to the great in yourself. Have no cares. You will obtain

rewards. Set out towards the south. Take action. This generates meaning and good fortune by releasing transformative
energy. Correct, discipline and put things in order. Your purpose is indeed on the move.

Transforming Lines

Initial six: You are permitted to ascend the mountain. Be
honest and true. This generates great good fortune and meaningful events by releasing transformative energy. Your purpose
is united with the higher powers. *Direction:* This inaugurates
a great and flourishing time. If you let yourself be led, you
can realize your hidden potential. The situation is already
changing.

Nine at-second: Connect with the spirits and put yourself in
order. Then take advantage of this situation by making an
offering, no matter how meagre your resources. You are in a
good position. You will have cause to rejoice. *Direction:* Keep
your words simple and connected to the facts. Release bound
energy. Obstacles will soon dissolve. The situation is already
changing.

Nine at-third: You ascend into an empty city. Don't stop now.
This isn't the time or place to have doubts. *Direction:* Organize
your forces and march on. Something significant is returning.
Be open to it. Provide what is needed.

Six at-fourth: The king offers sacrifices for the growth of the
people on the ancestral mountain of Ch'i. Dedicate your energy
to the good of the group. This generates meaning and good
fortune by releasing transformative energy. It is not a mistake.
It will certainly yield benefits for all. *Direction:* Continue on
the way you are going. Be resolute. You are connected to a creative force.

Six at-fifth: Put your ideas to the trial. This generates meaning
and good fortune by releasing transformative energy. Ascend
the steps to the seat of power. Your purpose will make great
gains. *Direction:* Secure the underlying structure by connecting

with common needs. Be resolute. You are connected to a creative force.

Six above: Dim ascending, dark and obscure, with no lights to guide you. Whether you are walking though a dark night, the cavern of the underworld or a forest of misinformation, don't stop. The only way to take advantage of this situation is to keep going through it. *Direction:* The situation is corrupt. If you let yourself be led out of it, you can realize your hidden potential. The situation is already changing.

47 Confining / Oppressed, K'UN

Keywords: Look within. Find a way to break out of the trap.

Confining/Oppressed describes your situation in terms of being cut off, oppressed and exhausted. The way to deal with it is to collect the energy to break out of the enclosure and re-establish communication. This is pleasing to the spirits. Through it they will give you success, effective power and the capacity to bring the situation to maturity. Be great and master the situation from within. Find what is truly important to you. Seek those who can help and advise you. This generates meaning and good fortune by releasing transformative energy. The situation is not your fault. Words are not to be trusted. There is a breakdown of communication and you are being isolated by it. You are not believed when you speak. Don't believe what others are telling you to do.

> **Confine/Oppression,** K'UN: Enclosed, encircled; restrict, limit; punishment, penal codes, prison; worry, anxiety, fear; fatigue, exhaustion, at the end of your resources; afflicted, disheartened, weary; poverty. The ideogram portrays a growing tree surrounded by an enclosure.

The hexagram figure shows outer relations disconnected from the inner flow. The mists are outside the stream. Find supportive people. Ascending without stopping has brought on confining. Hidden within the situation is the possibility of meeting unexpected help and encouragement. Use confining to separate your own power to realize *tao* from the collective values that are oppressing you. Bring old relations to an end and move toward new connections. Don't be bound by grudges or bitter feelings. Find the mandate for change hidden in this situation and use it to release a sense of your purpose. What is strong and solid is covered and hidden. It is dangerous to express yourself. Being confined and not letting go of yourself is pleasing to the spirits. Through it they will give you success, effective power and the capacity to bring the situation to maturity. This situation activates your connection to the *tao*. It can generate meaning and good fortune by releasing transformative energy. Seek those who can help you. Find what is great in yourself, your solid centre. You will not be believed when you speak. Finding value in what your oppressors tell you to do will only exhaust you.

Transforming Lines

Initial six: Buttocks confined, oppressed by a wooden rod. Punished or hurt, you enter into a dark valley, hiding yourself in deep melancholy. If you act like this you will be alone for three years. Retreat will not bring you understanding. *Direction:* Express yourself and join with others. Find a supportive group. Gather energy for a decisive new move.

Nine at-second: Confined and oppressed when drinking spirits and taking things in. This is the oppression of not being recognized. The badges of honour, luck and accomplishment are on their way. They are coming at you from all sides. Connect to the sources of inner energy. This brings profit and insight. Disciplining people or setting out on an expedition will cut you off from the spirits and leave you open to danger. Stay centred in your situation and you will be rewarded. *Direction:* Gather people and resources for a great new project. Proceed step by step. Gather energy for a decisive new move.

Six at-third: Your confinement is turning you to stone. Everything you touch turns to thorns and snares. You walk into your house and don't see your helpmate. This cuts you off from the spirits and leaves you open to danger. It is certainly not auspicious. *Direction:* A time of transition. Don't be afraid to act alone. You are connected to a creative force.

Nine at-fourth: Something is coming very slowly and quietly. When it drives up to your door, you will realize you have been going at things the wrong way. It will enable you to bring this oppression to an end. Stay low. Your situation is not appropriate. You will soon have people to associate with. *Direction:* When the right moment comes, take the risk. Nourish things. Take the situation in. Be open to new ideas.

Nine at-fifth: Your nose and feet are cut off. You are oppressed by authority. You will slowly find a way to express yourself in this situation. Connect to sources of inner energy. This brings profit and insight. You haven't found your purpose yet. Make straightening yourself out the centre of your concerns. Accept the situation as given and count your blessings. It could be much worse. *Direction:* Release bound energy. Your deliverance is on the way. The situation is already changing.

Six above: Confined and oppressed by vines and creeping plants. You are moving towards something hazardous in a stumbling and dizzy way. Don't blather on, stirring up all this anguish and repenting. You will be sorry in the end. Set things in order. Discipline yourself and others. Beginning to move generates meaning and good fortune by releasing transformative energy. *Direction:* State your case clearly and persuasively. Find a supportive group. Stay inside it. Gather energy for a decisive new move.

48 The Well,
CHING

Keywords: Communicate, connect, draw on the water.

The Well describes your situation in terms of an underlying social structure and the natural force that flows through it. The way to deal with it is to clarify and renew your connection to the source. The water is there for all to draw on. The well that gives you access to it must be cleaned and maintained. You can change where you live and who you associate with, but you can't change the well and the needs it represents. Losing and acquiring, coming and going, all are part of the well and its water. If all you find is mud in the well, you haven't gone deep enough. Your rope is too short. If you ruin the pitcher used to draw the water, you will be cut off from the spirits and left open to danger.

> **The Well,** CHING: A water well; the well at the centre of a group of nine fields; resources held in common; underlying structure; nucleus; in good order, regularly; communicate with others, common needs; the water of life, the inner source. The ideogram portrays a group of nine fields with the well at the centre.

The hexagram figure shows inner penetration flowing out into the world. Above the wood there is the stream. Turn potential conflict into creative tension. When what is above is confined, what is below is reversed. The well means interpenetrating and free communication. It is the earth in which the power to realize *tao* is grounded. It means staying where you are but shifting your ideas by differentiating what is right. Work for the common good at humble tasks to encourage fortunate meetings. Inner penetrating reaches to the stream and brings it to the surface. The well nourishes without being exhausted. You can change where you live, but you can't change the well. It is the solid centre. If you only bring up mud, your rope isn't long enough. You haven't achieved anything yet. If you ruin the pitcher used to hold the water, you will be cut off from the spirits and left open to danger.

Transforming Lines

Initial six: At present, this well is a bog. You can't take the water in. It is an old source that no creatures come to. Time has left it behind. *Direction:* Wait for the right moment to act. Turn potential conflict into creative tension. If you let yourself be led, you can realize your hidden potential. The situation is already changing.

Nine at-second: This well is a gully in which you shoot fish. The pitcher that holds the water is cracked and leaking. There is no possibility of associating with others by using this source. *Direction:* Re-imagine the situation. Gather your energy for a decisive new move.

Nine at-third: This well is turbid because it is not being used. Your heart aches, because your capacities are not being drawn on. The water could be used if the person in control were bright enough to understand the situation. This shows some-one of value unappreciated and under-employed. Although it hurts to move, seek out a situation in which your worth is recognized. This can bring blessings to all concerned. *Direction:* Take the risk. Provide what is needed. Be open to new ideas.

Six at-fourth: This well is being lined. Although the water can't be used, adjusting the source is not a mistake. *Direction:* This is a time of transition. Don't be afraid to act alone. You are connected to a creative force.

Nine at-fifth: There is cool, pure spring water flowing in this well. You can take it in. This source is central and correct. *Direction:* Make the effort. If you let yourself be led, you can realize your hidden potential. The situation is already changing.

Six above: This well receives everything and gives to every-one. Don't cover it up. Don't hide the source of value. You are linked to the spirits and they will carry you through. This is the source of great good fortune and meaningful events. You can accomplish great things. *Direction:* Gently penetrate to the core of the situation. Turn potential conflicts into creative tensions. The situation is already changing.

49 Skinning / Revolution, Ko

Keywords: Strip away the old. Revolt and renew.

Skinning/Revolution describes your situation in terms of stripping away the protective cover. The way to deal with it is to radically change and renew the way things are presented. Eliminate what has grown old and useless so that the new can be seen. You must wait for the right moment to act, when the snake is ready to shed its skin and the sun is approaching the zenith. When the right moment arrives, act with confidence. You will be linked to the spirits and they will carry you through. This begins a whole new cycle of time. All your doubts and sorrows will be extinguished.

Skin/Revolution, Ko: Take off the skin; moulting; change, renew; revolt, overthrow; prepare hides; skin, leather; armour, soldiers; eliminate, repeal, cut off, cut away. The ideogram portrays an animal skin stretched on a frame.

The hexagram figure shows changing awareness coming to expression. In the middle of the mists there is fire. You are coupled with a creative force. The way of the well and its deep waters has forced you to skin away the old. Skinning means to reject old motives, sorrows, memories and quarrels. Regulate the way you understand time in order to clarify when the right moment comes. Stream and fire come together for a moment. They are like two women who live together but have different purposes and desires. This is called skinning. Wait for the right moment. Act and trust what you are doing. You will be linked to the spirits and they will carry you through. Brighten the inner pattern by expressing it. You can promote great growth by correcting the situation. This is pleasing to the spirits. Skin and renew things. Your doubts and sorrows will be extinguished. Heaven and earth renew themselves and the four seasons accomplish things. Great people change and renew the mandate of heaven. Let yielding and serving connect you to heaven and mutual resonance connect you to the people. The time of skinning is truly great.

Transforming Lines

Initial nine: Bound with leather thongs. For now, you are held fast. It is impossible to put anything into action. *Direction:* Be open to the impulse when it comes. Don't be afraid to act alone. Take action. You are connected to a creative force.

Six at-second: This is the hour when the snake changes its skin. The time has come to revolt and renew things. Discipline and put things in order. Set out on an expedition. This generates meaning and good fortune by releasing transformative energy. It is not a mistake. Acting, moving, motivating things brings praise, glory and excellent results. *Direction:* Be resolute. Take action. You are connected to a creative force.

Nine at-third: Disciplining people and setting out on an expedition now will cut you off from the spirits and leave you open to danger. This is not the time to act. You are facing an angry old ghost who has returned to take revenge for past mistreatment. You must wait until you hear the words that call for revolution approach you three times. Then act with confidence. You will be linked to the spirits and they will carry you through. You will truly know what you are talking about. *Direction:* Follow the stream of events. Proceed step by step. Gather energy for a decisive new move.

Nine at-fourth: Act and have no doubts. All your regrets will disappear. You are linked to the spirits and they will carry you through. Change the mandates of heaven. Reform the fate of the people. This generates meaning and good fortune by

146

releasing transformative energy. Have complete faith in your purpose. *Direction:* The situation is already changing.

Nine at-fifth: When the mandate of heaven changes, great people transform like tigers. They move radically and abruptly from one state of being to another. Their fierce energy protects their followers. You are following a fundamental shift of ideas. Act with complete confidence, for you are linked to the spirits and they will carry you through. Don't bother to look for signs and omens. Your own inner pattern will brighten events. *Direction:* This ushers in a time of great abundance. Don't be afraid to act alone. Take action. You are connected to a creative force.

Six above: When the mandate of heaven changes, use the oracle to stay in touch with the *tao*. Transform yourself like a panther. Move from one state of being to another with grace, beauty and independence. Small people, who adapt to whatever crosses their path, will imitate this by changing their faces. Stay where you are. This generates meaning and good fortune by releasing transformative energy. Disciplining people or setting out on an expedition now would cut you off from the spirits and leave you open to danger. *Direction:* Gather people around you and give them a common purpose. This will couple you with a creative force.

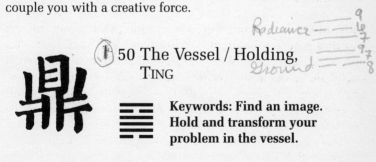

50 The Vessel / Holding, TING

Keywords: Find an image. Hold and transform your problem in the vessel.

The Vessel/Holding describes your situation in terms of imagination and the transformative capacity of a sacred vessel. The way to deal with it is to contain and transform your problem through an image. You need to see deeply into what your problem means. Security and a new beginning will come from this awareness. It is a time for reflection, for slowly turning and examining things. This is the origin of great good fortune and meaningful events. It releases transformative energy. It is pleasing to the spirits. Through it they will give you success, effective power and the capacity to bring the situation to maturity.

> **Vessel/Holding,** TING: A cauldron with three feet and two ears, a sacred vessel for cooking offerings, sacrifices and ritual meals; founding symbol of a family or dynasty; receptacle; hold, contain and transform, transmute; consecrate, connect with the spirits; found, establish, secure; precious, well-grounded. The ancient ideogram portrayed questioning the spirits.

The hexagram figure shows inner penetration feeding a spreading radiance and clarity. Above wood there is fire. Be resolute and break through inner obstacles. Once the old has been eliminated, there is nothing that can take the place of the vessel and its transformative power. Through the vessel you can grasp renewal. Correct the situation in order to give your fate a solid base. The vessel means making and using symbols, like fire uses wood. Offer something to the spirits through cooking it. The sage uses this kind of offering to present things to the supreme spirits above and to nourish wise and worthy people. This brightens the understanding of the ear and the eye and lets you see invisible things. What is flexible and adaptable advances and moves to the higher position. Through it you can acquire the centre and connect with what is solid and strong. This is pleasing to the spirits. It is the origin of success, effective power and the capacity to bring the situation to maturity.

Transforming Lines

Initial six: Turn the vessel upside down to get rid of an obstruction. Something is blocking communication and you will have to go outside normal channels to clear it. Getting out of this obstructed situation brings profit and insight. It is like taking a concubine when your wife can't have a child. This is not a mistake. It is not being rebellious. It is seeing and following what is valuable. *Direction:* This ushers in a great and creative time. Be resolute. Take action. You are connected to a creative force.

Nine at-second: There is food cooking in the vessel. You are contemplating something of real value. Think about who your companions are and how far you can trust them. Something near you is afflicted by sickness, disorder, anger or hate. But they can't approach you. Accept this separation. It generates meaning and good fortune by releasing transformative energy. Consider where you are going to place what you are cooking here. Bring your plan to completion without going to extremes. *Direction:* Search outside the norms. You may have to set out on a journey. Don't be afraid to act alone. You are connected to a creative force.

Nine at-third: Skinning the vessel's ears. Things feel all clogged up. You can't get a handle on what is happening. You can't get at the juice. Don't worry, this is part of a process that is changing and renewing how you understand things. Change is accumulating. It will fall like rain and wash away your doubts and sorrows. Bringing your plan to completion generates meaning and good fortune by releasing transformative energy. Don't be self-righteous. *Direction:* Gather energy for a decisive new move.

Nine at-fourth: Breaking off the vessel's foot. The action you are contemplating is wrong. Don't do it. You are in danger of severing what you stand on and spilling the contents all over the person who supports you. Everything will be soiled. It will cut you off from the spirits and leave you open to danger. Why betray a trust? *Direction:* This is a corrupt solution. If you let yourself be led out of it, you can realize your hidden potential. The situation is already changing.

Six at-fifth: This vessel has golden handles and metallic rings that let you transport it. Your plans are cooked. You have found the centre. Put your ideas to the trial. This brings profit and insight. *Direction:* Take action. It will couple you with a creative force.

Nine above: You have found something precious in the vessel, an idea that can orient and focus your life. This generates great good fortune and meaningful events by releasing transformative energy. There is nothing for which it will not, ultimately, be advantageous. It articulates a whole new world. Express it. Give it form and shape. *Direction:* Persevere. Be resolute. You are connected to a creative force.

51 Shake / Arousing, CHEN

Keywords: The shock of the new. Stir things up. Don't get flustered.

Shake/Arousing describes your situation in terms of a disturbing and inspiring shock. The way to deal with it is to rouse things to new activity. Re-imagine what you are confronting. Let the shock shake up your old beliefs and begin something new. Don't get flustered. Don't lose your depth and concentration. What at first seems frightening will soon be a cause to rejoice. This is pleasing to the spirits. Through it they will give you success, effective power and the capacity to bring the situation to maturity. The thunder rolls and everyone is frightened. You can hear them screaming in terror. Then the fright changes to joy and you hear everyone laughing and talking. The sudden shock spreads fear for thirty miles around. Don't lose your concentration. Hold the libation cup calmly so the dark wine arouses and calls the spirits.

Shake, CHEN: arouse, inspire; wake up, shake up; shock, frighten, awe, alarm; violent thunder clap (thunder comes from below in Chinese thought), earthquake, put into movement, begin; terrify, trembling; majestic, severe; *also:* Excite, influence, affect; work, act; break through the shell, come out of the bud. The ideogram portrays rain and the sign for exciting.

The hexagram figure shows repeated shocks that stir things up. Reiterating thunder. Re-imagine your situation. Nothing is better for putting a great idea into action than being the first child of thunder. Shake means stirring things up; it means beginning and undertaking things. Anxiously and fearfully inspect and adjust yourself. This is pleasing to the spirits. Through it they will give you success, effective power and the capacity to bring the situation to maturity. The shake comes and terrifies everyone. The anxiety it causes will ultimately bring blessings. When laughing words ring out, you will have what you need. The shake startles what is far away and frightens what is near. Don't lose your depth and concentration. When the shake comes from the earth, it is time to go out and attend to the ancestral temple, the field altar and the sacrifice to the gods of the growing crops. Act as master of the ceremonies that bring fertility.

Transforming Lines

Initial nine: The shake comes, terrifying everyone. Then laughing words ring out. This generates meaning and good fortune by releasing transformative energy. The anxiety caused by this impulse to action will bring you blessing in the end. It shakes everything up. Let it move you. After the fright, you will soon have what you need. *Direction:* Gather strength so you can react quickly when the impulse comes. Re-imagine your situation. Gather energy for a decisive new move.

Six at-second: The shake releases an angry old ghost who returns to take revenge for past mistreatment. A difficult time. You lose everything you think is valuable. Climb the mountain of transformation. Don't run after what you have lost. You will get everything back when the seventh day comes round again. You are riding a solid force. *Direction:* If you let yourself be led, you can realize your hidden potential. The situation is already changing.

Six at-third: The shake revives everything. Courage, strength, energy and good cheer return. Move with this impulse. It is not a mistake. You see things clearly. This situation is not appropriate for you. *Direction:* Moving will usher in a time of abundance. Don't be afraid to act alone. Take action. You are connected to a creative force.

Nine at-fourth: The shake releases a bog. This impulse to act will trap and confuse you. The situation is not clear yet. *Direction:* Something significant is returning. Be open to new ideas. Don't take the lead. Provide what is needed.

Six at-fifth: The shake comes and goes. The impulse to act is unsteady. This creates difficulty. It releases an angry old ghost that returns to take revenge for past mistreatment. If you can stay intent on your idea, you will have plenty to do. You are moving through danger and are in an exposed position. Keep what you must do your central concern. Your great idea will not be lost. *Direction:* Follow the stream of events. Proceed step by step. Gather energy for a decisive new move.

Six above: The power of the shake, the impulse to action, is exhausted in a net of demands and obligations. You watch this happening to those around you and are terrified at the prospect. Don't try to discipline people and put things in order. You will be cut off from the spirits and left open to danger. Don't let this directly affect you. Let it affect your neighbours and watch what is happening. That is not a mistake. You will hear words proposing marriages and alliances. Beware. You haven't found the centre of things yet. Though there is a trap in this situation, you can avoid getting caught in it. Let what happened to your neighbours be a warning to you. *Direction:* Bite through the obstacle you are confronting. Re-imagine the situation. Gather energy for a decisive new move.

52 Bound / Stabilizing,
Ken

Keywords: The time comes to an end. Calm, still, stabilize, articulate.

Bound/Stabilizing describes your situation in terms of recognizing a limit, or coming to the end of a cycle. The way to deal with it is to calm and stabilize your desire to act in order to understand what has been accomplished. Calm yourself. Don't try to advance. See through your desire. By doing this you stabilize yourself in the world of the spirits and allow them to emerge. Quiet your body. Calm and stabilize your back. This stills your personality so it is not caught up in compulsive actions. Move through your life as if the people were not there. This is not a mistake. It allows you to stabilize and articulate yourself.

> **Bound/Stabilizing**, Ken: Limit, boundary, obstacle; still, quiet, calm, refuse to advance; enclose, mark off, confine; finish, complete; reflect on what has come before; firm, solid, simple, straightforward; the mountain as a limit and a refuge; *also:* Stop, bring to a standstill. The ideogram portrays an eye and a person turning around to see what has led up to the present situation.

The hexagram figure shows the limit of things. Joining mountains. Recognizing this limit releases you from compulsive action. You can't stir things up forever. You must also stop them. Bound means stopping. Think over things deeply and don't leave your current situation. Stopping means stabilizing. When the time comes to an end, stop. When the time moves, move. Stir things up or quiet things down without letting go of the right time to move. Then your *tao* will shine brightly. Bound means stopping yourself. Stopping means staying in your place. What is above and what is below in this situation are connected only through antagonism. They do not meet and associate. Don't get your personality entangled in things. By moving through your life as if the people were not there, you will free yourself from error and make no further mistakes.

Transforming Lines

Initial six: Calm and stabilize your feet. Take no action. Make your foundation firm. This is not a mistake. You will create a source of continuing advantage, profit and insight. *Direction:* Beautify things. Release bound energy. The situation is already changing.

Six at-second: Calm and stabilize your calves. Stop moving. You will not be able to rescue the people who are following you. They run on at any cost. Your heart does not rejoice at this. But don't stop listening to your inner voice. *Direction:* The situation is corrupt. If you let yourself be led out of it, you can realize your hidden potential. The situation is already changing.

Nine at-third: Trying to calm and stabilize things, you freeze your hips and lower back. You cut yourself in half. This releases an old angry ghost that returns to take revenge for past mistreatment. Acrid smoke rises. Your heart is smothered by the difficulties. This is not the way to put things in order. *Direction:* Strip away these old ideas and open yourself to new ones. Don't take the lead. Provide what is needed.

Six at-fourth: Calm and stabilize your body and your personality. This is not a mistake. It frees you from errors. This means stopping your body's compulsive actions. *Direction:* Separate yourself from social groups. Don't be afraid to act alone. You are connected to a creative force.

Six at-fifth: Calm and stabilize your jaws. Then the words you speak will have order and proceed directly from inner ideas. All your doubts and regrets will be extinguished. Make correcting one-sidedness and excess your central concern. *Direction:* Proceed step by step. Gather energy for a decisive new move.

Nine above: Calm and stabilize the situation through honesty and generosity. Be magnanimous. This generates meaning and good fortune by releasing transformative energy. Use these qualities to bring your plans to completion and you will meet them in others. *Direction:* Keep your words simple and connected to the facts. Release bound energy. You will be delivered from your problem. The situation is already changing.

53 Infiltrating / Gradual Advance, CHIEN

Keywords: Proceed smoothly, step by step. Don't take control.

Infiltrating/Gradual Advance describes your situation in terms of gradually achieving a goal. The way to deal with it is to advance slowly and steadily through subtle penetration. Move through the woman and the yin. Through infiltrating, you find the place where you belong. Proceed step by step, and don't try to dominate the situation. This generates meaning and good fortune by releasing transformative energy. You will ultimately achieve mastery and find a new field of activity. Put your ideas to the trial. This brings profit and insight.

Infiltrate/Gradual Advance, CHIEN: Advance by degrees, little by little, slowly and surely; reach, pour into, flow into; moisten, permeate; influence, affect; smooth, gliding. The ideogram portrays the penetrating quality of water.

The hexagram figure shows an inner limit that stabilizes outer growth. Above the mountain there is a tree. Gather energy for a decisive new move. You can't just stay in one place. Infiltrating means advancing. Be like a woman given in marriage who gives priority to the man's initiative. Depend on your moral and intellectual strength and your power to realize the *tao* to improve the everyday situation. This will certainly advance you. By moving through yin and the woman you achieve mastery and a new field of activity. You acquire the place you desire. Pushing on brings real achievement. Correct yourself in order to advance. This lets you correct the way power and responsibility is assigned. You will acquire a solid place in the centre. Stabilize your desire and be adaptable. Gently penetrate to the core of the situation. Thus the new energy that is stirring will not be exhausted.

Transforming Lines

Initial six: The wild geese advance to the river bank. The bird of the soul emerges. A new relationship begins. You are like a young child confronting difficulties. There is an angry old ghost here who has returned to take revenge for past mistreatment. Use words to deal with it. You are not making a mistake. Act as the young son of the family. You will be righteous and just. *Direction:* Gather energy for a decisive new move.

Six at-second: The wild geese advance to the huge stone. The soul finds a foundation. The relationship is grounded in happiness. There is eating and drinking, a feast in which everyone rejoices. This generates meaning and good fortune by releasing transformative energy. Don't just gratify yourself. *Direction:* Gently penetrate to the core of the situation. Turn potential conflict into creative tension. The situation is already changing.

Nine at-third: The wild geese advance to the high plateau. The soul is cut off and loses its way. The husband is punished and does not return. The wife is pregnant and gives no support. The relationship breaks down in mutual recriminations. Whether you are a husband or a wife, acting like this will cut you off from the spirits and leave you open to danger. Firmly resist the temptation to be violent and brutal. That brings profit and insight. A husband who acts like this is a drunken fool. A wife who acts like this is letting go of who she is. Yield and work together for your mutual protection. *Direction:* Step back and contemplate the situation. Let everything come into view. Strip away old ideas and be open to new ones. Provide what is needed.

Six at-fourth: The wild geese advance to the trees. Perhaps you acquire a roof over your head. This is a good temporary solution. It is not a mistake. By yielding and serving you can adapt to the situation. *Direction:* Soon you will have to retire. Don't worry or try to hang onto things. You are coupled to a creative force.

Nine at-fifth: The wild geese advance to the grave mound. The soul seeks out the images of its past. The couple asks advice of the ancestral spirits. The wife will not conceive for three years. Finding the solution to this problem will take a while. Don't try to complete things too quickly. It is definitely worth the time and effort. This generates meaning and good fortune by releasing transformative energy. In the end nothing will hold you back; you will acquire the place you want. *Direction:* Stabilize your desire. Release bound energy. Your deliverance is coming. The situation is already changing.

Nine above: The wild geese advance to the high plateau. Their feathers can be used in the rites and dances that connect you with the fundamental powers. This generates meaning and good fortune by releasing transformative energy. The journey comes to an end in the symbolic world. Everything finds its place. *Direction:* Re-imagine your situation. Gather energy for a decisive new move.

54 Converting the Maiden, Kuei Mei

Keywords: Realize hidden potential. Let yourself be led.

Converting the Maiden describes your situation in terms of a change you must go through which is beyond your control. You are not the one who has chosen. The force involved is larger than you are. The way to deal with it is to accept it and let yourself be led. You cannot escape the situation. It reflects a deep and unacknowledged need. It is moving you towards a new field of activity, the place where you belong. Don't try to discipline people or take control of the situation. That will cut you off from the spirits and leave you open to danger. Don't impose your will, have a plan or a place to go. Being free of such plans will bring you profit and insight. This is a very special situation that, in the long run, can lead to great success.

Convert, KUEI: Come back to, go back to, return to; change form, turn into; restore, revert, become loyal, give back; belong to; to give a young girl in marriage. The ideogram portrays a woman who becomes head of a household.

Maiden, MEI: A young girl, a virgin; the younger or second sister. The ideogram portrays a woman and the sign for not yet.

The hexagram figure shows self-expression cheerfully following rousing new energy. Above the mists there is thunder. The situation is already changing. In order to advance you must have a way to convert your hidden potential. Bring this potential to completion through the woman and the yin. Don't try to dominate the situation. Adapt and provide what is needed. By bringing everything to completion you will understand what is unfit to be used. Converting the maiden is the great righteousness of heaven and earth. If heaven and earth did not mingle like this, the myriad beings would never emerge. For the maiden, this is both an end and a beginning. Stir up expression and pleasure. This is the way to convert the maiden. Punishing people or imposing your will cuts you off from the spirits and leaves you open to danger. It is not the right situation to do that. Don't make plans or impose directions. Be supple and adaptable and ride on the strong, solid force.

Transforming Lines

Initial nine: Converting the maiden as a second wife. A lame person is able to make their way and earn a living. You are installed in a secondary position. Accept it cheerfully. It will enable you to go your way. Discipline and set things in order. Set out on an expedition. This generates meaning and good fortune by releasing transformative energy. Persevere in this position. By acting together with your superior you receive gifts, commands and benefits. *Direction:* Release bound energy. Your deliverance is on its way. The situation is already changing.

Nine at-second: By squinting at things you will be able to see them. Take an independent perspective. Looking at things from solitude and obscurity brings profit and insight. The rules aren't changing yet. *Direction:* There is a fertile shock on the way. Re-imagine the situation. Gather energy for a decisive new move.

Six at-third: Converting the maiden through waiting. Have patience. If you accept a secondary position now, you will turn the whole situation upside down. The time is not appropriate yet. *Direction:* Strengthen your position. Be resolute. You are connected to a creative force.

Nine at-fourth: The agreed date for converting the maiden has gone by. Don't panic. Delay and act at your leisure. This will connect you with the way time is moving. Wait for the right moment, then act. But don't be idle within yourself. *Direction:* A significant connection is approaching. It is the return of something important. Be open to new ideas. Don't take the lead. Provide what is needed.

Six at-fifth: The great ancestor gives a maiden in marriage. This is an omen of future happiness and success. What comes from the womb of the first wife is not as fine as what comes from the womb of the second wife. Be like the moon that is almost full. That generates meaning and good fortune by releasing transformative energy. Historically, this is the story of the end of one ruling family and the beginning of another. Accept being in a secondary position. You are located in the centre of things. Value your ability to move and act on your ideas. *Direction:* Express yourself and join with others. Find a supportive group. Stay inside it. Gather energy for a decisive new move.

Six above: A woman offers a basket with nothing in it. A man sacrifices a goat with no blood. This is a sterile situation; these are empty forms. There is no advantage in this situation. There is nothing honest or sincere at the top. *Direction:* Turn potential conflict into creative tension. The situation is already changing.

55 Abounding, FENG

Keywords: Shine on everything. Give with no cares.

Abounding describes your situation in terms of abundance and fertile profusion. The way to deal with it is to be exuberant and expansive. Overflow with good feeling, support and generosity. Give with both hands. This is pleasing to the spirits. Through it they will give you success, effective power and the capacity to bring the situation to maturity. Imagine yourself as the king whose power bestows wealth and happiness on all. Rid yourself of sorrow, melancholy and care. Be like the sun at midday. Shed light on all and eliminate the shadows.

> **Abounding,** FENG: Abundant harvest; fertile, plentiful, copious, numerous; exuberant, prolific, at the point of overflowing; fullness, culmination; ripe, sumptuous, luxurious, fat; exaggerated, too much; have many talents, friends, riches. The ideogram portrays an overflowing vessel and sheaves of grain, a horn of plenty.

The hexagram figure shows brightness and warmth permeating the world and stirring up growth. Thunder and lightning bring everything to culmination. Assemble all your force. Don't be afraid to act alone. Acquiring a field of activity means having a great idea. Abounding refers to your great idea. Many things have brought you to this point, among them quarrels and sorrows. Cut through legal arguments and let punishment take place. Brightness and awareness stir everything up. This is the source of abounding. Imagine yourself as a king whose power confers benefits on everyone. Honour what is great. Rid yourself of all sorrow and melancholy. Shed your light on everything below heaven. When the sun reaches the centre, it begins to set. When the moon becomes full, it begins to wane. Heaven and earth fill and empty all things. There is a time to associate with others and build things up, and a time to let structures dissolve so the new can emerge. This is even more true of people and of the souls and spirits that govern the world.

Transforming Lines

Initial nine: You meet your lord as an equal. This is a very fortunate meeting with someone who can help and teach you. You can continue with this relation for a whole period of time. This is not a mistake. Going on brings honour and rank. You will surpass yourself. When the time is over, leave or face disaster. *Direction:* Be very careful with the beginnings. Don't be afraid to act alone. You are connected to a creative force.

Six at-second: Abounding screens you off and protects you. At noon you can see the Northern Bushel, the great star constellation. Your position enables you to see things that others cannot. If you act directly on this insight, you will be distrusted and injured. Have confidence in your connection to the spirits. They will carry you forward and display your worth. This generates meaning and good fortune by releasing transformative energy. Trust in the connection to the inner world to display your purpose. *Direction:* Rouse your strength and make your purpose firm. Be resolute. You are connected to a creative force.

Nine at-third: Abounding spreads and flows in all directions. At noon, you can see the heavens full of stars. You break your right arm. This is an influx of extraordinary perception. You are caught up in such a profusion of events you can't tell the inner from the outer. You lose the capacity to act directly. This is not your fault. It is not a mistake to yield to the profusion. You will not be able to do great things or bring your project to completion. *Direction:* The fertile shock of a new time is on its way. Re-imagine your situation. Gather energy for a decisive new move.

Nine at-fourth: Abounding screens you off and protects you. At noon you can see the Northern Bushel, the great star constellation. Your position enables you to see things that others cannot. In this profusion you meet your lord in hiding. This is an important connection with someone who can help and teach you. It generates meaning and good fortune by releasing transformative energy. Your situation is not appropriate. You are being kept in the shade. Take action to change it. This will generate meaning and good fortune by releasing transformative energy. *Direction:* Accept the difficult time that is coming. It will release bound energy and deliver you from your problems. The situation is already changing.

Six at-fifth: The coming composition, whether this is something you are making or chapters in the book of life, will bring you praise and rewards. It will generate meaning and good fortune by releasing transformative energy. *Direction:* Change the way you present yourself and renew the time. You are coupled with a creative force.

Six above: Abounding under a roof. Screening off your dwelling. Peeping through the door. You are using your abundance to cut yourself off from other people. This cuts you off from the spirits and leaves you open to danger. If you go on like this, you will be isolated and alone. You won't see another person for three years. You are so proud your head touches the sky. What are you trying to conceal? *Direction:* Become aware of yourself. Gather your force and leave this situation. Take action.

56 Sojourning / Quest,
Lü

Keywords: Journeys, voyages, searching alone and outside.

Sojourning/Quest describes your situation in terms of wandering, journeys and living apart. The way to deal with it is to mingle with others as a stranger whose identity and mission come from a distant centre. You are outside the normal network, on a quest of your own. Be small and flexible. Adapt to whatever crosses your path. This is pleasing to the spirits. Through it they will give you success, effective power and the capacity to bring the situation to maturity. Be willing to travel and search alone. Put your ideas to the trial. This generates meaning and good fortune by releasing transformative energy.

> **Sojourn/Quest,** Lü: Travel, journey, voyage; stay in places other than your home; temporary; visitor, lodger, guest; a troop of soldiers on a mission; a group (of travellers) that hold things in common or have a common goal; a stranger in a strange land. The ideogram portrays people gathered around a banner, loyal to a symbol of something distant.

The hexagram figure shows an inner limit that stabilizes changing awareness. Above the mountain, there is fire. Don't be afraid to act alone. If your ruling idea is exhausted, you must let go of where you live. Use your travels to connect solitary individuals. Brighten and consider things. Don't be held up by complications. Make clear decisions even if they are painful. Being small and adapting to what crosses your path is pleasing to the spirits. What is supple and flexible is moving to the centre in the outer world. By yielding and working with it, you connect with what is solid and strong. Limit and stabilize your desire when you join with others. This makes you aware of things. It is why being small is pleasing to the spirits. Be willing to travel and search alone. Put your ideas to the trial. This generates meaning and good fortune by releasing transformative energy. The time of sojourning is truly and righteously great.

Transforming Lines

Initial six: The voyage breaks up into little pieces. The traveller annoys everyone with trivialities. You are being obnoxious and your thinking is petty. You will lose what security you have, be seized by disaster and ruined. Your purpose will be exhausted before you start. Do you really want to act like this?

Direction: Become aware of yourself. Don't be afraid to act alone. You are connected to a creative force.

Six at-second: The traveller approaches a resting place. This is a camp open to all, so take care of your goods. Cherish those who depend on you. You will acquire a young helper, someone who can aid you in putting your ideas to the trial. Bring your plan to completion without going to excess. *Direction:* You can imaginatively transform your situation and found something significant. Be resolute. Take action. You are connected to a creative force.

Nine at-third: The traveller burns down the resting place and loses the young helper. This is a difficult time. You are facing an angry old ghost who has returned to take revenge for past mistreatment. There is real injury involved. Don't get pulled into the conflict. Don't be self-righteous. *Direction:* Don't be frightened. You will slowly and surely emerge into the light of day. Re-imagine the situation. Gather energy for a decisive new move.

Nine at-fourth: The traveller is established in a stable position. You obtain goods, an office and the signs of respect, everything that a traveller would dream of acquiring. But your heart is not happy or satisfied. You haven't found yourself in this situation yet. Even with all the outward signs of honour, you are troubled. *Direction:* Stabilize your desire and realize the limits. Release bound energy. Your deliverance is on its way. The situation is already changing.

Six at-fifth: Take aim and shoot at what you want. This is the goal of your quest. You are aiming at something clever and beautiful that is probably above you and well defended. If you can get it, you can put yourself in order. If the first effort fails, don't be discouraged. You will succeed in bringing your plan to completion. You will acquire praise and a mandate to carry out. *Direction:* When you have what you need, retire from the situation. You are coupled with a creative force.

Nine above: The bird burns and destroys its nest. Travellers laugh at first, then burst out crying. Do not act on your plan!

It might seem at first that it will bring you joy, but it will unquestionably lead to disaster. You will lose all your property and the place where you rest. This will cut you off from the spirits and leave you open to danger. You are acting above yourself. Your own self-righteousness will defeat you. *Direction:* Be extremely careful. Don't be afraid to act alone. You are confronting a dangerous force.

57 Ground / Penetrating, SUN

Keywords: Gently penetrate to the core of the problem.

Ground/Penetrating describes your situation in terms of the pervasive influence of the ground from which it grows. The way to deal with it is to penetrate to the core of the problem by being supple and adaptable. Enter from below. Let the situation shape you. Be humble and compliant; adapt to whatever crosses your path. Take the pervasive action of the wind, or growing plants extending their roots and branches as your model. This is pleasing to the spirits. Through it they will give you success, effective power and the capacity to bring the situation to maturity. Hold on to your purpose. Have a place to go. Impose a direction on things. See great people. Seek out those who can help and advise you. Think about the great in yourself and how you organize your thoughts. All these things bring profit and insight.

Ground/Penetrating, SUN: Support, foundation, base; penetrate, enter into, put into; supple, mild, subtle, docile, submissive; submit freely, be shaped by; *also:* Wind, weather, fashion; wood, trees, plants with growing roots and branches. The ideogram portrays things arranged on a base that supports them.

The hexagram figure shows subtle penetration over time. Following winds. Turn potential conflict into creative tension.

If you are travelling and don't have a place of your own, this means subtly penetrating from outside. It means being humble and hiding your virtues. Ground pares away what is unnecessary to realizing the *tao*. Evaluate things in private. Balance and equalize opposing forces. Carry out what you have been told to do. What is solid and strong has reached the centre. It is correcting things and its purpose is moving. Be supple and adaptable in order to yield and work with the strong. That is why adapting to what crosses your path is pleasing to the spirits. Have a place to go. Impose a direction on things. See great people. Seek out those who can help and advise you. Think about the great in yourself and how you organize your thoughts. All these things bring profit and insight.

Transforming Lines

Initial six: In advancing and retreating, being supple doesn't mean being indecisive. You may have to change directions many times. Whichever direction you take, be firm. Be a warrior. If you are indecisive, you will needlessly doubt your own purpose. Putting your ideas to the trial through decision and strength will remedy that. It will bring profit and insight and make you fit to take charge. *Direction:* Accumulate small things to achieve something great. Turn potential conflict into creative tension. The situation is already changing.

Nine at-second: Penetrate beneath the bed. Get to the core of this old story. Use shamans and read old histories. Find out what it is and bring it to light, however confused it might be. This generates meaning and good fortune by releasing transformative energy. It is not a mistake. You can get to the centre of the problem. *Direction:* Proceed step by step. Gather energy for a decisive new move.

Nine at-third: Penetrating and pushy. You are making incessant demands. Don't go on like this. It leads to shame and humiliation. Your purpose will be exhausted. *Direction:* Disperse illusions. Let the light shine through. Take the situation in. Be open to new ideas. Don't take the lead. Provide what is needed.

Six at-fourth: Whatever you are contemplating, do it. All your regrets will disappear. When you hunt you will catch three kinds of game. You will get everything you want. You are in a position to achieve something solid. *Direction:* You are coupled with a creative force.

Nine at-fifth: Put your ideas to the trial. This generates meaning and good fortune by releasing transformative energy. All your doubts and regrets will vanish. There is nothing for which this will not, ultimately, be advantageous. Don't try to bring your plans to completion too quickly. Take three days to prepare before the fruit emerges, and three days afterwards to make sure things are in order. *Direction:* There is something corrupt in this situation. Find the source. Realize the hidden potential. The situation is already changing.

Nine above: You are trying to penetrate beneath the bed and get to the core of an old problem. Stop. Don't go any farther. If you go on like this, you will lose your goods and your position. By putting your ideas to the trial you will be cut off from the spirits and left open to danger. You have taken your attempt to correct things too far. You have reached the top and you are exhausted. *Direction:* Connect with others through your common needs. Turn potential conflict into creative tension. The situation is already changing.

58 Open / Expressing, TUI

Keywords: Express yourself. Join with others. Persuade, inspire, enjoy.

Open/Expressing describes your situation in terms of communication, pleasure and exchange. The way to deal with it is express yourself openly and interact with others. Cheer people up and urge them on. Talk, bargain, barter, exchange information. Enjoy yourself and free others from constraint.

This is pleasing to the spirits. Through it they will give you success, effective power and the capacity to bring the situation to maturity.

> **Open/Expressing,** TUI: Open surface, interface; interact, interpenetrate; express, persuade, stir up, urge on, cheer, delight; pleasure, pleasing, enjoy; responsive, free, unhindered; meet, gather, exchange, barter, trade; pour out; the mouth and the words that come from it; *also:* Mists, vapour rising from a marsh or lake; fertilize, enrich. The ideogram portrays a person speaking.

The hexagram figure shows expression and interaction between people. The mists come together. Find a supportive group. Stay inside it. When you penetrate something, you must rouse it to action. Open means stimulating things through expression. It means being visible and visiting people. Join with friends to discuss and practise things. What is strong and solid is in the centre. What is supple and adaptable is outside. Put your ideas to the trial through expressing them and urging people on. That way you both yield and serve heaven and connect with others for mutual benefit. If you explain things to people before they set to work, they will forget how hard the labour is. If you explain why something is difficult and oppressive, they will even face death willingly. By explaining the central idea, you encourage people at their tasks.

Transforming Lines

Initial nine: Harmonizing through expression. Bring things together. Make peace. Unite and adjust. This generates meaning and good fortune by releasing transformative energy. Act without doubts. *Direction:* This will lead you out of isolation. Find a supportive group. Stay inside it. Gather energy for a decisive new move.

Nine at-second: Through expressing your ideas you are linked to the spirits and they will carry you through. This generates meaning and good fortune by releasing transformative energy. Trust your purpose. *Direction:* Follow the stream of events. Proceed step by step. Gather energy for a decisive new move.

Six at-third: An opportunity to express yourself and persuade others is coming towards you. Beware! This is not the right opening for you. If you act, you will be cut off from the spirits and left open to danger. This situation is not appropriate. *Direction:* Be resolute. Take action. You are connected with a creative force.

Nine at-fourth: Express yourself through deliberating, bargaining and arguing. You have not yet reached an agreement in this matter. Rigorously guard against anger, hatred and disorder, all the sudden emotional afflictions that would distort your judgement. This brings rejoicing and reward. *Direction:* Articulate your ideas. Take things in. Don't try to dominate the situation. Provide what is needed.

Nine at-fifth: Strip away your old ideas. This will link you to the spirits and they will carry you through. You are confronting an angry old ghost that has returned to take revenge for past mistreatment. Correcting the situation is definitely the appropriate thing to do. *Direction:* If you let yourself be led, you can realize your hidden potential. The situation is already changing.

Six above: Draw things out by expressing your ideas. The situation isn't clear yet. Make your way carefully. *Direction:* Find a supportive group. Stay inside it. Gather energy for a decisive new move.

59 Dispersing,
HUAN

Keywords: Clear away what is blocking the light.

Dispersing describes your situation in terms of the possibility of eliminating misunderstandings, illusions and obstacles. The way to deal with it is to clear away what is blocking clarity and understanding. Scatter the clouds, melt the ice, dispel fear and illusions, clear up misunderstandings, eliminate suspicions.

Let the fog lift and the sun shine through. This is pleasing to the spirits. Through it they will give you success, effective power and the capacity to bring the situation to maturity. Be like the king who imagines a temple full of images that unite people and connect them with greater forces. This is the right time to embark on a significant enterprise or to enter the stream of life with a purpose. Put your ideas to the trial. That brings profit and insight.

> **Disperse,** HUAN: Scatter clouds, break up obstacles; dispel illusions, fears and suspicions; clear things up, dissolve resistance; untie, separate; change and mobilize what is rigid; melting ice, floods, fog lifting and clearing away. The ideogram portrays water and the sign for expand. It suggests changing form through expanding or scattering.

The hexagram figure shows fluid movement gently penetrating the world. The wind moves above the stream. Take things in and provide what is needed. When something is expressed it scatters and spreads clarity. This is dispersing. Dispersing means that the light shines through. The early kings used this time to make offerings to the highest powers and establish temples. Dispersing pleases the spirits; through it they will give you success, effective power and the capacity to bring the situation to maturity. What is solid and strong keeps coming without being exhausted. What is supple and flexible acquires the outer situation and connects with the strong above. Be like the king who imagines a temple full of images that connect with greater forces. This is the right time to embark on a significant enterprise or to enter the stream of life with a purpose. Make ready your vehicle, the boat that will carry you, and go on to achieve something solid.

Transforming Lines

Initial six: Someone or something is in trouble. Rescue them with the invigorating strength of a horse. Be the knight in armour. This generates meaning and good fortune by releasing transformative energy. Yield to the impulse and produce results. *Direction:* This is a deep and sincere connection. Take things in. Provide what is needed.

Nine at-second: Disperse the obstacles by leaving what you are leaning on. Let go of your habitual support. By doing this you will acquire what you desire. *Direction:* Let everything come into view and find the central meaning. Strip away your old ideas and be open to new ones. Provide what is needed.

Six at-third: Scatter the obstacles by dispersing your identification with your body. Don't let your desires or your need to express yourself get in the way of what you are doing. Have no doubts about this. Locate your purpose outside yourself. *Direction:* Gently penetrate to the core of the problem. If you let yourself be led, you can realize your hidden potential. The situation is already changing.

Six at-fourth: Disperse your flock, the usual group of people or thoughts that you gather around you. This is the source of great good fortune and meaningful events. It releases transformative energy. By dispersing those who usually surround you, you will be able to see the hilltop shrine used to worship the spirits. Go there, but not simply to hide yourself. It will give you a chance to ponder what is really significant. A great idea will come shining through. *Direction:* When the new time comes, present your position directly and convincingly. Find a supportive group. Stay inside it. Gather energy for a decisive new move.

Nine at-fifth: An order from on high, a great outcry. Sweat this one out. The king is moving his residence and you are part of the project. This is not a mistake. It will correct your situation. *Direction:* You don't understand the situation yet. Take things in. Be open to new ideas. Provide what is needed.

Nine above: Dispersing blood. Remove the possibility of conflict. Send your valuables far away. By leaving the situation you emerge from the difficulties. This is not a mistake. Keep harm at a distance by removing temptations. *Direction:* Take the risk. You are facing a dangerous situation that you cannot avoid. Take things in. Be open to new ideas. Provide what is needed.

60 Articulating,
CHIEH

Keywords: Articulate your thoughts. Set limits. Give things rhythm and form.

Articulating describes your situation in terms of the relations between things. The way to deal with it is to articulate and make the connections clear. Express your thoughts. Separate and distinguish things. Make chapters, sections, units of time. Create a whole in which each thing has its place. This is pleasing to the spirits. Through it they will give you success, effective power and the capacity to bring the situation to maturity. But don't harm yourself or others. Rules that are bitter and harsh will prevent you from putting your ideas to the trial.

> **Articulate,** CHIEH: Separate, distinguish and join things; express ideas in speech; joint, section, chapter, interval, unit of time, rhythm; the months of the year; limits, regulations, ceremonies, rituals, annual feasts; measure, economize, moderate, temper; firm, loyal, true; degrees, levels, classes. The ideogram portrays the nodes or joints on a stalk of bamboo.

The hexagram figure shows expression articulating the stream of events. Above the mists is the stream. Take the situation in and provide what is needed. Things can't simply spread out. They must be articulated. Articulating means holding things in. Cut things to size and calculate the measures. Think about what realizing the *tao* means before taking action. Articulating is pleasing to the spirits. Through it they will give you success, effective power and the capacity to bring the situation to maturity. Apportion the supple and the solid. Keep the strong at the centre. Harsh limits will prevent you from putting your ideas to the trial. Your *tao* will be exhausted. Express things, take action, take risks. This is the right time to articulate your situation. Correct excess, stay in the centre and communicate with others. Heaven and earth articulate and the four seasons accomplish their aims. By using articulating to shape the measures and the times, property will not be injured and the people will not be harmed.

Transforming Lines

Initial nine: Don't leave the house. This restriction is not a mistake. Stay inside your own world for now. In this way you will understand when you can connect with others and when communication is blocked. *Direction:* You are facing a dangerous situation. Eventually you will have to act. Take things in. Be open to new ideas. Provide what is needed.

Nine at-second: If you don't step outside the way you usually act and think, you will be cut off from the spirits and left open to danger. The time is coming to an end. You are letting the opportunity slip through your fingers. *Direction:* A new time is beginning. Help everything find a place to grow. Strip away your old ideas and be open to new ones. Provide what is needed.

Six at-third: If you don't articulate things and set limits, you will always be mourning over painful memories. Think about it. This is not a mistake. Whose fault is all this confusion and sorrow? *Direction:* Wait for the right moment to act. Turn potential conflict into creative tension. The situation is already changing.

Six at-fourth: Peacefully and quietly articulate your ideas. This is pleasing to the spirits. Through it they will give you success, effective power and the capacity to bring the situation to maturity. *Direction:* Express yourself and inspire others. Find a supportive group. Gather energy for a decisive new move.

Nine at-fifth: Articulate your ideas sweetly, with delight and grace. Avoid bitterness, anger or recrimination. This generates meaning and good fortune by releasing transformative energy. Going on in this way brings honour, esteem and recognition. Stay in the situation and move to the centre. *Direction:* A significant connection is approaching. It is the return of something important. Be open to new ideas. Provide what is needed.

Six above: Harsh measures and bitter speech. Whatever it is, don't do it. Putting these ideas to the trial will cut you off from the spirits and leave you open to danger. Have no doubt about it. Your *tao* will be exhausted. *Direction:* First connect your inner and outer life and find an accord with the spirits. Take the situation in. Be open to new ideas. Provide what is needed.

61 Centring Accord, CHUNG FU

Keywords: Connect your inner and outer life. Be in accord with the spirits.

Centring Accord describes your situation in terms of the need to bring your life into accord with the spirits. The way to deal with it is to make connecting the inner and the outer parts of your life your central concern. Be sincere, truthful, reliable. Make your inner vision and your outer circumstances coincide. Empty your heart so you can hear the inner voices. Act through these voices with sincerity and honesty in connecting with others. This will link you to the spirits and they will carry you through. Swim like a dolphin in the stream of the way. This generates meaning and good fortune by releasing transformative energy. This is the right time to enter the stream of life with a purpose, or to embark on a significant enterprise. Put your ideas to the trial. That brings profit and insight.

Centre, CHUNG: Inner, central, calm, stable; put in the centre; balanced, correct; mediate, intermediary, between; the heart, the inner life; stable point that lets you face outer changes. The ideogram portrays an arrow fixed in the centre of a target.

Accord, FU: Accord between inner and outer; sincere, truthful, verified, reliable, worthy of belief; have confidence; linked to and carried by the spirits; take prisoners, capture spoils, be successful. The ideogram portrays a bird's claw enclosing a young animal. It suggests both being protected and making a successful capture.

The hexagram figure shows inner expression permeating the outer world. Above the mists is the wind. Take the situation in and provide what is needed. Articulate and trust yourself. Centring Accord means being trustworthy. Think about legal actions before getting involved and put off serious judgements. Be flexible and adaptable within so the strong can acquire the centre. Expression and penetration will link you to the spirits and let you change the way power and responsibility is assigned. Be like the dolphin, who swims the seas of the way. Commit yourself to the waters. This generates meaning and good fortune by releasing transformative energy. This is the right time to embark on significant enterprises. Ride in an empty wooden boat. Put your ideas to the trial. That brings profit and insight and connects you with heaven above.

Transforming Lines

Initial nine: Taking precautions generates meaning and good fortune by releasing transformative energy. Stay alert and vigilant. Concentrate your attention. If you are always thinking about someone else, you will never be at ease. Your purpose isn't transforming yet. *Direction:* Dispel tensions and illusions. Take the situation in. Provide what is needed.

Nine at-second: A crane calls out from its hiding place. The young son echoes the cry. I have a loving cup. Come to me and I will pour it out. This is the profound echo of one soul to another, calling out from hiding and inviting to a hidden feast. This connection transforms your heart's desire. Don't hesitate to answer the call. *Direction:* A very fertile time is coming. Increase your efforts. Strip away your old ideas. Be open to the new. Provide what is needed.

Six at-third: You acquire an antagonist, an equal and opposed force. You beat the drums to sound the attack, then you call for a cease-fire. You weep, then you laugh. There is very little you can do in this situation. It is not really appropriate for you. *Direction:* Accumulate small things to achieve something great. Turn potential conflict into creative tension. The situation is already changing.

Six at-fourth: The moon is almost full. Cut yourself off from your team. This is not a mistake. By separating yourself and going your own way for now, you can connect with higher energies. *Direction:* Make your way step by step. Turn potential conflict into creative tension. Gather energy for a decisive new move.

Nine at-fifth: Act on your ideas. You are linked to the spirits and they will carry you through. This will connect you with others as surely as links in a chain. This is not a mistake. It is the right time to correct your present situation. *Direction:* Diminish your present involvements to make energy available for the new. Curb your anger. Something significant is returning. Be open to new ideas. Provide what is needed.

Nine above: The cry of a bird mounts to the heavens. This is nothing but empty talk. Putting your ideas to the trial this way will cut you off from the spirits and leave you open to danger. Why go on like this? *Direction:* Set limits and articulate your desires. Take things in. Be open to new ideas. Provide what is needed.

62 Small Exceeding, HSIAO KUO

Keywords: Carefully adapt to each thing. Keep your sense of purpose.

Small Exceeding describes your situation in terms of a seemingly overwhelming variety of details. The way to deal with it is to carefully adapt to each thing in turn. Be very careful and meticulous. Adapt conscientiously to whatever comes. This is pleasing to the spirits. Through it they will give you success, effective power and the capacity to bring the situation to maturity. Put your ideas to the trial. That brings profit and insight. The time allows you to do small things. It does not allow you to do great things. The flying bird leaves this message behind: the above is not suitable, the below is suitable. Don't go up, go down. This generates great good fortune and meaningful events by releasing transformative energy. Keep your sense of purpose. Don't look to others to solve your problems.

Small, Hsiao: Little, common, unimportant; adapt to what crosses your path; take in, make smaller; dwindle, lessen; little, slim, slight; yin energy.

Exceed, Ku: Go beyond; pass by, pass over, surpass; overtake, overshoot; get clear of, get over; cross the threshold, surmount difficulties; transgress the norms, outside the limits; too much.

The hexagram figure shows an inner limit restricting new energy. Above the mountain there is thunder. Don't be afraid to act alone. If you have found something to trust you must move it. Through being very small you can move beyond. When you are active, be excessively polite. When you are mourning, be excessively compassionate. When you are paying, be excessively frugal. Being small is pleasing to the spirits. Through it they will give you success, effective power and the capacity to bring the situation to maturity. Putting your ideas to the trial brings profit and insight. The flexible and adaptable acquires the centre. Small matters generate meaning and good fortune by releasing transformative energy. What is strong and solid has lost its central position. Great matters are not allowed. This is truly the symbol of a flying bird who leaves a message behind: the above is not suitable, the below is suitable. Don't go up, go down. This generates great good fortune and meaningful events by releasing transformative energy. Above you will be thwarted. Stay below. That yields results.

Transforming Lines

Initial six: The bird tries to fly and falls into a pit. Don't act like this. You will be cut off from the spirits and left open to danger. This kind of action is simply not allowed by the time. *Direction:* A time of abundance is coming. Gather your energy. You are connected to a creative force.

Six at-second: Pass your grandfather by and meet your grandmother. You won't reach the chief but meet the servant. Don't try to push your demands. Staying below and working from a secondary position is not a mistake. Be a servant. Don't push yourself forward. *Direction:* Acting like this has enduring value. Be resolute. It connects you to a creative force.

Nine at-third: This plan will put you in an exposed and perilous position. All you can do is defend yourself. If you keep on, you risk death. This cuts you off from the spirits and leaves you open to danger. Don't act. *Direction:* Gather strength so you are ready when the real call to action comes. Re-imagine your situation. Gather energy for a decisive new move.

Nine at-fourth: Acting like this is not a mistake. You will meet the object of your desire. Let the difficulties that are now passing away be a warning to you. Don't keep trying to find new ways to stay in the same place. This situation is not appropriate for you. When you find what you need, you won't be able to stay. *Direction:* Keep your words humble and connected to the facts. Release bound energy. Your deliverance is on its way. The situation is already changing.

Six at-fifth: The dense clouds are rolling in from the west, but the rain hasn't arrived yet. The duke shoots a string-arrow and connects with someone in hiding. In a situation of building tension, you connect with a hidden force. This is a climax and an enduring connection to a higher power. *Direction:* Be open to this influence. It couples you with a creative force.

Six above: You won't meet what you want by doing this, you will pass it by. You are acting like the flying bird who keeps on going, leaving the earth far behind. Don't do it. You will be cut off from the spirits and left open to danger. You invite calamity from within and without. This is truly being overbearing. *Direction:* Step outside the situation. Don't be afraid to act alone. It will connect you with a creative force.

63 Already Fording,
CHI CHI

**Keywords: Stay in the process.
The situation is already changing.**

Already Fording describes your situation in terms of an action that is already underway. The way to deal with it is to actively go on with what you are doing. You are in the middle of fording the stream of events. Things are already in their proper places. Adapt to whatever crosses your path. Give aid and encouragement. This is pleasing to the spirits. Through it they will give you success, effective power and the capacity to bring the situation to maturity. Put your ideas to the trial. That brings profit and insight. Stay with the process. That generates meaning and good fortune by releasing transformative energy. Trying to bring things to completion creates disorder. Remain underway.

> **Already,** CHI: Completed, finished; mark of the past tense; thus, that being so. The ideogram portrays a person kneeling in front of a bowl of food, already having begun the meal.

> **Ford,** CHI: Cross a river, overcome an obstacle, begin an action; give help, bring relief; succeed, bring to a successful conclusion, complete. The ideogram portrays water running over a flat bottom, a shallow fording place.

The hexagram figure shows clarity in action. The stream is above the fire. Things are cooking. Keep gathering your energy and put it at the service of the action underway. Having gone past the midpoint, you are now fording the stream. This means setting things right. Think deeply about problems and sorrows. Prepare to defend against them. Adapt to whatever crosses your path. This is pleasing to the spirits. Through it they will give you success, effective power and the capacity to bring the situation to maturity. Put your ideas to the trial. That brings profit and insight. You are in the right place. Correct the balance between what is supple and adaptable and what is strong and solid. Stay in the process. That generates meaning and good fortune by releasing transformative energy. Through being adaptable you acquire the central position. Completing things, and thus stopping the action, creates disorder. Your *tao* will be exhausted if you do that.

Transforming Lines

Initial nine: Whoa! Pull your wheels back. Get your tail wet. You are starting too quickly. Let things soak in. This is not a mistake. It is the right thing to do. *Direction:* Re-imagine the situation. Gather your energy for a decisive new move.

Six at-second: A wife loses the veil that screens her and hides her identity. Something valuable has been lost, but in the process something equally valuable will be revealed. Don't chase what is gone. In seven days you will have it back again. Stay in the centre and connect with the *tao*. *Direction:* Wait for the right moment to act. Turn potential conflict into creative tension. The situation is already changing.

Nine at-third: The great ancestor subdues demons on all sides. It will take him three years to control their country. This is a great enterprise that will take a long time to complete. In the process you will have to confront your own ghosts and shadows. Don't use small people and don't be adaptable. Keep your focus even though you are weary and distressed. *Direction:* This is a new beginning. Give everything a place to grow. Strip away your old ideas. Be open to new ones. Provide what is needed.

Six at-fourth: Watch out! Even silk clothes can become rags in a single day. You are crossing the river in a leaky boat and may have to use your finery to stop a leak. Be constantly on guard. You have good reason for doubt. *Direction:* Change the way you present yourself. Renew the time. This will couple you with a creative force.

Nine at-fifth: The eastern neighbour sacrifices a bull. The western neighbour makes a small but sincere offering. Don't compare yourself with the rich and don't be ostentatious. Timing and sincerity are important here. By being true to yourself you will receive the gifts of the spirits. Great good fortune and meaningful events are on their way. Be sincere and keep your focus. *Direction:* Accept the difficult time. Release bound energy. Your deliverance is on its way. The situation is already changing.

Six above: You soak your head. You are in too deep and have lost yourself. You are confronting an angry old ghost that has returned to take revenge for past mistreatment. You are not in the position to deal with it. Why let this go on? *Direction:* Find a supportive group. Stay inside it. Gather energy for a decisive new move.

64 Not Yet Fording, WEI CHI

Keywords: Gather your energy for a decisive new move.

Not Yet Fording describes your situation in terms of being on the verge of an important change. The way to deal with it is to gather your energy to make this decisive new move. You are about to launch a plan, cross the river or overcome an obstacle. The possibilities are great. Be sure your plans are in order and that you have accumulated enough energy to make the crossing without getting stuck. This is pleasing to the spirits. Through it they will give you success, effective power and the capacity to bring the situation to maturity. Don't be like the small fox that gets almost across the river and then soaks her tail in the mud of the opposite shore. That would leave you with nowhere to go and nothing to do that would help you.

Not Yet, WEI: Incomplete, doesn't exist yet; has not occurred (but will occur in the course of time). The ideogram portrays a tree that has not yet extended its branches.

Ford, CHI: Cross a river, overcome an obstacle, begin an action; give help, bring relief; succeed, bring to a successful conclusion, complete. The ideogram portrays water running over a flat bottom, a shallow fording place.

The hexagram figure shows the potential for order. Fire is located above the stream. Things aren't cooking yet. But they are moving towards their proper place. Life cannot be exhausted. The potential is always there. That is the meaning of not yet fording. It implies diminishing masculine drive. Carefully consider and distinguish all the beings that surround you. Gathering your energy for a decisive new move is pleasing to the spirits. Through it they will give you success, effective power and the capacity to bring the situation to maturity. By being supple and adaptable you can acquire the central position. The small fox who crosses a river to the muddy shores beyond never lets go of her centre. If you start out, then soak your tail, there is no plan or direction that can help you. Don't end the movement, continue it. You aren't in the right place yet. But what is supple and what is strong and solid are acting in harmony to move you towards where you belong.

Transforming Lines

Initial six: You soak your tail. Too much, too soon. This brings shame and regrets. If you act this way, you will show everyone that you don't really understand. *Direction:* Turn this potential conflict into creative tension. The situation is already changing.

Nine at-second: Pull your wheels back. Start slowly and carefully. Putting your ideas to the trial in this way generates meaning and good fortune by releasing transformative energy. Stay in the centre and correct how you are moving. *Direction:* You will slowly and surely emerge into the light. Release bound energy. Your deliverance is on its way. Gather yourself for a decisive new move.

Six at-third: You are getting ready to cross the river, preparing for a decisive new move. Don't discipline and punish people or set off on an expedition to put things in order. That will cut you off from the spirits and leave you open to danger. Step into the stream of life with a purpose. Embark on a significant new enterprise. That brings profit and insight. *Direction:* Ground and secure yourself in the imaginative world. You can found something significant. Be resolute. You are connected to a creative force.

Nine at-fourth: Put your ideas to the trial. This generates meaning and good fortune by releasing transformative energy. All your doubts and regrets will vanish. Rouse and inspire your forces. Invade the demon's country. After three years of hard work you will be honoured and rewarded in the capital. This is a great project that will take a long time to bring to fruition. In the process you will have to confront your own ghosts and shadows. In the end you will be recognized and rewarded. Your purpose is truly moving. *Direction:* You don't really understand the situation yet. Something significant is returning. Be open to it. Provide what is needed.

Six at-fifth: Put your ideas to the trial. This generates meaning and good fortune by releasing transformative energy. You will have no cause to regret it. Your connection to the way is shining through it. Your plan is linked to the spirits and they will carry you through. You will be splendid in your good fortune. *Direction:* Present your ideas clearly and persuasively. Find a supportive group. Gather energy for a decisive new move.

Nine above: Act on your plan with confidence. You are linked to the spirits and they will carry you through. Gather with others and drink in celebration. This is not a mistake. But don't soak your head and lose yourself. You will lose the ability to articulate your ideas. What will link you to the spirits is to stop doing that. *Direction:* Release bound energy. The situation is already changing.

FURTHER READING

The most comprehensive translation now available in English:
Karcher, Stephen and Ritsema, Rudolf, *I Ching: The Classic Chinese Oracle of Change*, Element Books, Shaftesbury, 1994

A classic study:
Wilhelm, Hellmut, *Heaven, Earth and Man in the Book of Changes*, University of Washington Press, Seattle, 1977

A comprehensive list of books on the *I Ching*:
Hacker, Edward A, *The I Ching Handbook*, Paradigm Publications, Brookline, 1993

On Chinese thought about the *I Ching*:
Peterson, Willard, 'Making Connections: Commentary on the Attached Verbalizations of the Book of Change', *Harvard Journal of Asiatic Studies*, 42/1, pp 67–112, June 1992

On divination:
von Franz, Marie Luise, *On Divination and Synchronicity: The Psychology of Meaningful Chance*, Inner City Books, Toronto, 1980

A look at the depth psychological approach:
Jacobi, Jolande, *Complex/Archetype/Symbol*, Princeton University Press, Princeton, 1974

On Chinese history and traditional culture:
Granet, Marcel, *Chinese Civilization*, Routledge, London, 1930

Maspero, Henri, *China in Antiquity*, trans. Frank A Kierman, University of Massachusetts Press, Amherst, 1978

The classic Neo-Confucian translation with an introduction by C G Jung:
Wilhelm, Richard and Baynes, Cary F, trans., *The I Ching or Book of Changes*, 3rd edition, Princeton University Press, Princeton, 1967

An interesting new translation of the oldest parts of the book:
Jing-Nuan, Wu, *Yijing*, Taoinist Study Series, Washington DC, 1991